DEATH PENALTY

Original Story & Screenplay
by

Michael Selsman

McNae, Marlin & Mackenzie
Book and Periodical Publishers
Glasgow   New York   Los Angeles
Queens Road, Glasgow, Lanarkshire G42 8OO Scotland

www.m3publishers.com

DEATH PENALTY

Copyright © 2018 by Michael Selsman.   All rights reserved.

Printed in the United States of America and in the United Kingdom by McNar, Marlin and MacKenzie, Ltd.

Except as permitted by the United States Copyright Act of 1976, no part of this publication may be reproduced, stored in a retrieval system or transmitted, in any form or by any means, electronic, mechanical, photocopying, recording, or otherwise without the prior written permission of the author or the publisher.

ISBN-13: 978-1-64316-120-4
ISBN-10: 1-64316-120-2

Reg: WGAW-1051704

michaelselsman@gmail.com

Visit us at www.m3publishers.com

DEATH PENALTY

Original Story & Screenplay
by

Michael Selsman

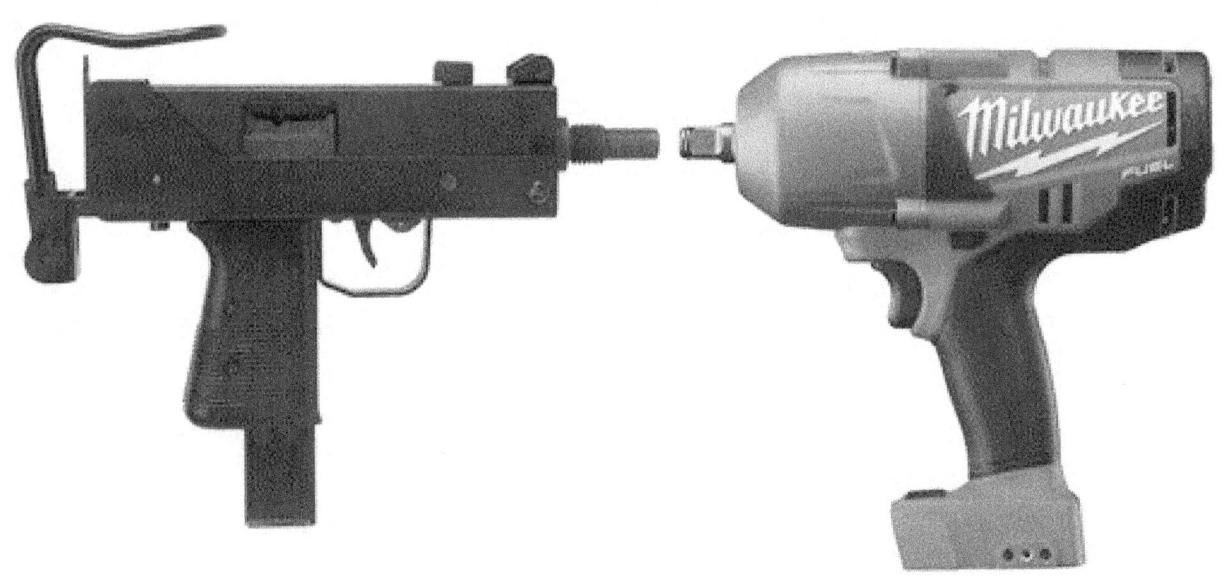

FADE IN:

EXT. NIGHT - SNOWING AND BITTER COLD

CAMERA PANS a semi-rural area - large, upscale mansions gaily decorated for CHRISTMAS occupy multi-acre lots.

STOP on IMPOSING GATES guarded by TWO MEN. One checks out occupants of an entering LIMO. As gates swing OPEN, FOLLOW car to front of brightly-lit HOUSE.

DISSOLVE TO: INT. LIVING ROOM - SAME - Warm and cheery - fireplaces blaze. STRING QUARTET softly plays Schubert. Fifty formally dressed GUESTS mingle, eating, drinking, laughing. SERVANTS pass trays of canapés and champagne.

TINKLE OF A BELL announces dinner - guests searching for their place cards file to festive tables scattered from dining room through loggia to glassed, heated patio. DANCE BAND replaces string quartet.

Chairs scrape floor as guests sit. CAMERA roams, STOPS at table, at which a large, florid, balding MAN of around 60, VINCENT GANDOLFO, STANDS, tapping his glass for silence.

Seated next to him is his family; MARY, SR., 40, his pretty wife, and daughter, MARY, JR., 21, attractive, intellectual. Others at the table include WILLIAM "BILLY" RUBIN, mid-30's, Vince's attorney. Handsome, with an unruly shock of black hair. His largish, slightly curved nose betrays his Eastern European heritage. Next to him, sits RAY GRECO, a contemporary of Vince's. Ray is short and fat, his custom-made tux failing to make a gentleman out of him. Ray's wife, GRACE, and their son, TONY, about 25, flank him. ROSE RUBIN, Billy's mother, a woman in her late fifties, occupies the remaining seat. She carries an air of sadness even at this festive occasion.

                           VINCE
Merry Christmas, everybody. Thanks for coming out on this cold night.

MURMURS, CALLS FROM GUESTS:

        A tradition, Vince...we're your family....We love you...nothing could keep us away".

                           VINCE
                       (genuinely moved)
You bring great honor on my house. (smiles) I want to make an announcement.

He looks the room over, then around his table.

                         VINCE (cont.)
I have set the wedding date for my daughter, Mary, to marry Anthony, the son of my good friend, Ray Greco.

CHEERS FROM THE AUDIENCE

CUT TO: VARIOUS CU's:

MARY, JR. - Dismay - She looks quickly at her mother.

PULL BACK TO INCLUDE MARY, SR. - Can't face her - looks away, masking her feelings.

ON TONY - Grinning lifts his glass to Vince.

ON BILLY - His face impassive.

MED. WIDE - Tony's mother, Grace, leaves her chair, goes to Mary Sr., still seated, hugs her from behind, then goes to Vince, gives him a big smooch. Vince, embarrassed, pulls back, motions for Ray to join him. They stand together, glasses raised.

> VINCE & RAY
> To our children's happiness and to a new and even more successful business future for both our families.

LOUD TOASTS, CHEERS - BAND BEGINS TO PLAY

CAMERA PANS VINCE'S TABLE - MONTAGE:

Mary, Jr., holding back her emotions, stands, walks quickly off. Tony doesn't even notice until, after a discreet moment, Billy stands, smiles down at his mother, and leaves in the same direction as Mary Jr.

Tony frowns.

FOLLOW BILLY THROUGH HOUSE INTO KITCHEN.

Controlled CHAOS: Large, professional catering STAFF busy cooking, loading plates, waiters stacking them on trays, etc.

Mary Jr. weaves her way through the bodies to back porch door, goes through. In a moment, Billy follows her.

EXT. SAME –

The snow has stopped. The cold black silence is eerie. Billy watches Mary Jr. as she shakes with silent sobs.

MARY, JR.

What am I going to do?

BILLY
(takes off his suit jacket, drapes it around her)
You mean we, don't you?

MARY, JR.

Billy, you're such a dreamer. Why aren't you afraid of him? I am! You know what he can do.

BILLY

I'm not worried. Look, Mary, you're his only child. You mean more to him than anything else in the world. He wants you to be happy.
(holds her close)
I think of Vince as my father, too. He and my dad were friends since they were little kids. It was Vince who sent me to law school and when Morrie died, gave me the only job I've ever had.

MARY, JR.

Billy, I love you…I've loved you since I was a little girl, because you're so different. But you don't understand them. You're not "family"...you could never be...don't you see...Vince and Ray, they're dinosaurs…meat-eaters. They belong to another culture…the old country.

She breaks away...pulls the jacket closer as she shivers. Looks up at a momentary break in the clouds to a few stars.

MARY JR. (cont.)

They made a deal…years ago. It's all about honor. Tony and I are part of it. (sighs) There's no escape.

BILLY

Sure there is. We're gonna' change all that, tonight, after the party. He'll understand when we talk to him together.

MARY, JR. (cont.)
(takes off Billy's jacket, shakes her head wearily)
Give me a couple of minutes...

She turns toward kitchen door, turns back, grabs him, buries her face in his chest.

MARY JR. (cont.)

We're both gonna' wish we were dead...you know that, don't you?

She goes back into kitchen. Billy's look of concern slowly changes to determination.

CUT TO: LATER THAT EVENING - INT. LIVING/DINING AREA

VARIOUS SHOTS:

Most of the guests have gone home. Band packs up. A few close associates linger, talking, smoking cigars. Mary Sr., and several WIVES, shoes off, gossip; small CHILDREN sleep on chairs and loveseats. Catering staff cleans up.

ANGLE:

Closed door to Vince's office. Several MEN sit outside on side chairs, talk in low tones.

ANGLE INSIDE - LOW LIGHT

POV from behind Mary, Jr. and Billy. They stand, holding hands, in front of Vince's desk. Between their two bodies we glimpse Vince, seated in a pool of yellow light from a spotlight above him, eyes lowered, quietly playing with a judge's gavel and brass-placqued base.

INSERT: The wall behind Vince is covered with photos of Vince with judges, politicians and sports figures.

> MARY, JR. (V.O.)
> Daddy, can mom come in?

> VINCE
> (softly)
> No, sweetheart. I don't think she'd like to hear what you're gonna' say. Whadda' you think…am I right?

> BILLY
> Vince...

> VINCE
> In time, counselor. Right now, I wanna' hear from my daughter.

> MARY, JR.
> (takes a breath)
> Daddy, I love you very much, and I know you want what's best for me...

Vince looks up, stares at the knot his daughter and Billy's hands make…then up at them.

MARY, JR. (cont.)
I'm a modern girl, daddy. I have an advanced degree. I want to work, to accomplish something…to be my own person....

ON VINCE - He bites his lower lip, looks down again, plays with his gavel.

MARY, JR. (cont.)
I don't love Tony. I'm sorry…I don't even like him. I understand the tradition, but I can't marry him and have his babies.

She breaks off from Billy, goes around desk to her father, kneels in front of him, pleads.

MARY, JR. (cont.)
Please, daddy, let me be what I can be.

Vince runs his manicured fingers gently over his daughter's hair.

VINCE
Sure, baby. I understand. You're my kid…you have your own ambitions, just like I did when I was your age. Now, stand up.

She does, goes towards Billy again.

VINCE (cont.)
No, sit there, on the couch. I want to hear the rest from my lawyer.

BILLY
Vince, Mary's in agony. And so am I. We both love you, but we love each other also.

VINCE
Really...how long has this been goin' on?

He looks at Mary, Jr.

MARY, JR.
Daddy, I've loved Billy since I was ten years old.

BILLY
Mary came to me a year ago, told me you were planning her marriage to Tony. She was distraught, frightened…she felt she couldn't talk to you or her mother about it.

VINCE
And you comforted her, is that it?

BILLY
I counseled her, Vince, as a professional.

MARY, JR.
(leaps in)
It was my fault, daddy. We spent time together...he knows me since I'm a baby, I trust him...like you do

VINCE
Not exactly like I do. Where'd this all happen...under my roof?

BILLY
Vince, don't make it sound like that.

VINCE
(his hooded eyes)
Like what? She's not a virgin anymore, right?

He looks at Mary, Jr., whose eyes lower to the carpet. She takes a breath, then;

MARY, JR.
Daddy, we want to get married as soon as possible.

VINCE
As soon as possible. I see. Mary, please excuse us, I want to talk to Billy alone. Go to your room. I'll be up later.

Mary, Jr. and Billy exchange looks. She rises, goes to door, looks back, gently closes the door behind her.

ON VINCE

VINCE
This is a sad day, Billy. You know who I feel sorry for more than any of us...? Morrie...your dad.

He gets up, walks around room, behind Billy.

VINCE (cont.)
We grew up together, always in trouble. I went to jail, he went to college, an accountant. One smart Jew-boy. As soon as I started makin' it, there was no stoppin' us. He couldn't support your mother and you doin' payroll taxes for shoe stores.

                          BILLY
                (nervous, can't see Vince behind him)
            He always told mom and me you were like brothers.

                          VINCE
                    (in the dark, only his voice)
            Yeah, we were. I didn't wanna' put you on the payroll, but he insisted. Said it would
            be good for the business. I trusted him with my life. When he died, I had a special
            rosary said for him by a bishop. My whole family went. He woulda' laughed...I miss
            him...

Suddenly, Vince reappears in the light, in front of Billy.

                          VINCE (cont.)
            So let me understand. You knocked up my kid...

                          BILLY
            Please, Vince, it's not like that...

                          VINCE
            My virgin daughter is gonna' have a kike kid...my plans to combine my operation
            with Greco's is in the shitter now, wouldn't you say, counselor?

FROM BEHIND HIS BACK, he whips out the gavel he's been holding and smashes Billy in the face with it, drawing a huge amount of blood. Shocked, Billy throws his hands to his face as Vince, out of control, continues to beat him to the ground.

ANGLE OUTSIDE THE DOOR. The men outside listen, look at each other, continue smoking their cigars.

BACK INSIDE VINCE'S OFFICE

Billy is in a heap, bleeding into the rug. Vince kicks him heavily in the stomach.

                          VINCE
            Traitor...Jew-bastard.
                              (yells out)
            Augie!

OUTSIDE

One of the men jumps up, enters.

BACK INSIDE

> VINCE
> (disgust)
> Take my "lawyer" down to the basement. I'll be down later…figure out what to do with him.

AUGIE jerks his head toward the others looking in; they pick up Billy and remove him. Augie takes out his silk breast pocket handkerchief, tries to mop up some of the blood.

CUT TO:

BLACK SCREEN

SOUNDS - Someone moaning...footsteps stumbling…crashing into a wall, something slumps to the floor.

SCREEN LIGHTENS

CAMERA finds Billy's beaten form.

The DOOR - SOUND of a key turning in lock –

C.U. - HANDLE TURNS

PAN UP AS MARY, JR'S FACE PEEKS IN

ON HER as she silently goes to him, closing door behind her.

TWO-SHOT:

Signaling silence, she helps him up. Gesturing toward the stairs, draping Billy's arm around her shoulder, they quietly exit.

CUT TO: EXT. NIGHT – SAME - STILL SNOWING - WIND HAS PICKED UP

FROM A DISTANCE:

Billy, alone and shivering, dressed only in suit pants and bloody shirt, walks unsteadily down deserted country road. HE STOPS - looks around...

C.U. - FEAR on his face - are those headlights? Satisfied it's only reflections, he turns away and staggers on.

CUT TO: EXT.

EARLY NEXT MORNING - DOWNTOWN PROVIDENCE, R.I.

Snow has STOPPED - PLOWS ROAR by, heaping piles on parked cars. WORKERS make their way through the mess. CAMERA focuses on impressive facade of FEDERAL BUILDING

CUT TO: INT. BUILDING - FIFTH FLOOR

Glass double doors bear legend - FEDERAL BUREAU OF INVESTIGATION

In front of doors, a ragged MAN curled up, sleeping. REVERSE ON ELEVATOR DOORS OPEN discharging group of FBI EMPLOYEES.

REACTIONS

ANGLE ON

A tall, brush-haired, middle-aged, mustachioed MAN, CHARLES DRAGO, SAC, pushes through, squats down, checks life signs.

                DRAGO (straightens up)
Hurt bad...passed out. (to secretary) Get Gary and Phil to bring him in.
My office.

Drago goes through double doors.

CUT TO:

INT. DRAGO'S OFFICE – LATER - TWO-SHOT

                DRAGO
You're one hustler I never expected to see in my office.

Cleaned up, but black and blue and wearing someone else's shirt, Billy sits drinking coffee, smoking a cigarette.

                BILLY
Choosing between the FBI and the Charles River wasn't hard.

                DRAGO
Either way, you're a dead man.

BILLY
(starts to stand)
Oh, well, in that case...

DRAGO
(smiles)
Sit down...you want to see a doctor?

BILLY
Yeah, I would...nothing's broken, but I want some prescriptions.

DRAGO
Sure...well, what can we do for you, counselor?

BILLY
(gives him an incredulous look)
Protection. What else are you good for?

DRAGO
(now a smirk)
You'll testify?

BILLY
Do I have a choice? Didn't you just call me a dead man?

DRAGO
You should know. You're going to live with me until the trial...they won't touch a federal agent. After that, you'll be in the Witness Protection Program. Anyone you want to contact?

BILLY
Just my mother…and…

DRAGO
(waits)
And...

BILLY
(slowly shakes his head)
That's it.

Drago rings for his secretary.

                        DRAGO
            Willy...we need a set-up.

CUT TO: EXT. FEDERAL COURTHOUSE - PROVIDENCE – DAY

SHOTS of POLICE LINES around entrance –

OFFICERS holding back CROWDS of media and onlookers.

CRUISERS arrive escorting white VAN with smoked windows, disappearing into building garage.

CUT TO: LINCOLN LIMO pulling up at curb. Doors open –

FOCUS ON Vince Gandolfo, his lawyer, BERNARD LYNCH, Ray and Tony Greco exit. Vince smiles, nods at cameras, ignores yelled questions, enters building.

INT. COURTROOM

ON BAILIFF

                        BAILIFF
            All rise!

SRO AUDIENCE shuffles to their feet

 POV - JUDGE ENTERS, SITS, ARRANGING PAPERS, ETC.

                        BAILIFF (cont.)
            Judge Irving Mellinger presiding. Docket number U.S.-239…United States versus
            Vincent Gandolfo, Raymond Greco, Roberto D'Antoni, Gaetano Scallini, etc. al.
            Please be seated.

AUDIENCE BUZZES

                        MELLINGER
                  (peers over his glasses)
            Counsels?

ON PROSECUTOR'S TABLE

WENDY LEVIN - early 40's, pretty, and smart.

                    LEVIN
            The government is ready, Your Honor.

ON DEFENSE

Lynch - handsome, silver-haired; despite his name, he's Jewish.

                    LYNCH
            Ready for the defense, Your Honor.

                    MELLINGER
            Call your first witness, Ms. Prosecutor.

Levin nods to bailiff.

                    BAILIFF
            The State calls William Rubin.

ANGLE ON SIDE DOOR

Billy emerges, goes directly to witness stand, avoids looking at Vince's table or the audience.

                    BAILIFF
            Raise your right hand.

ANGLE INTO AUDIENCE

Tony Greco - His hateful stare bores into Billy. Seated next to him is Mary, Jr., visibly pregnant.

C.U. - FRONT PAGE - PROVIDENCE TIMES - BOLD HEADLINE: "GANDOLFO, GRECO CONVICTED, FACE LONG TERMS FOR MURDER"

CUT TO:

INT. DRAGO'S FBI OFFICE - TWO-SHOT

                    DRAGO
            You want a new face…or just a new name…or both?

                    BILLY
            (smiles, touches his nose)
            You mean the feds have a plastic surgeon on the payroll?

DRAGO
We can arrange it. Your friends are never gonna' forget you.

BILLY (thinks a minute)
Thanks. I'll keep my face. What about a name?

DRAGO
What do you want to be called?

BILLY
You mean I get to choose…you don't assign me a name?

DRAGO
That's right. You live with it, you might as well be happy.

BILLY
I see. Where am I going to live?

DRAGO
Wherever you want.

Billy thinks a moment.

BILLY
I've always liked the name "Ed"…Let's see…How about "Ed Laborteaux"

DRAGO
That's a strange one…where'd you get it?

BILLY
I read a lot of history. He was a general, a hero in the French-Indian War.

DRAGO
Hero, huh…I didn't know you had a sense of humor.   Here…
(pushes a pad towards him)
Write it out for me.

BILLY
(as he prints out his new name)
I want to live in Southern Arkansas, along the river…a little town called El Dorado.

DRAGO
What the hell for? I know that area…it's hot, humid, Mosquitoes as big as Volkswagens. What is a "gourmet" like you gonna' eat?

                          BILLY
Great fishing. I like to fish...I can hide pretty good there. And I like grits.
Don't you?

On Drago's look:

                          BILLY (cont.)
Who will know where I am?

                          DRAGO
Me...And a couple other agents on a "need to know" basis.   Don't worry, we
run a lot of heroes in Witness Protection.

EXT. SMALL AIRPORT – DAY

A private Lear jet lands, taxis past two-story tower bearing large sign - "WELCOME TO EL DORADO, ARKANSAS"

FOLLOW as it parks near a Chevy van drawn-up at the end of the field.

ANGLE: Jet door OPENS;

Drago steps out first, followed by a handcuffed Billy, then another MAN carrying two suitcases. They wear suits and ties.

ON VAN - Both front doors OPEN.

TWO MEN emerge and go to plane. They are dressed in country casual - chinos, cowboy boots, shirts and hats.

                          DRAGO
                     (to first man)
Butler?
                          BUTLER
                     (holds out his hand)
Yeah, you Drago?

                          DRAGO
                     (nods, shakes)
My partner is Gil Alberts, and here's your target.
                     (to Billy)
Introduce yourself…I can't ever get it right.

                              BILLY
        Ed L'Aborteaux.

                              BUTLER
        That's a good one. This here's your other keeper, Hank Pierce.

DRAGO takes keys from pocket, unlocks Billy's cuffs. Alberts takes paperwork from his breast pocket, offers it to Butler.

                              ALBERTS
        Sign here for safe delivery.

ON BUTLER as he signs.

                              DRAGO (to Billy)
        Now, life would be perfect if I never heard of you again. Think you can do that for me?

                              BILLY
        What if I catch the biggest crappie they've ever seen around here? Bound to make the news.

                              DRAGO
        Let me just close up with a word of advice, hustler. These crackers down here don't have your sense of humor. If you want to live to a ripe old age, you'd better try to blend in.

Billy smiles, rubs his free wrists.

MED. SHOT - Drago and Alberts re-board jet. Door CLOSES, and engines begin to WHINE.

ON BILLY AND HIS HANDLERS getting into van, driving away.

INT. VAN – SAME - POV FROM BEHIND BILLY in back seat.

                              BUTLER
                       (turned around to face him)
        Questions?

                              BILLY
        Some. What do I live on?

BUTLER

You get eight hundred a month, in cash. Either Pierce or me will give it to you in person. We'll come to you.

BILLY

Eight hundred a month? Can you live on that…what's the rent?

BUTLER

This ain't New York, or wherever you're from. Rent's paid. So are utilities. No telephone. I'd suggest makin' your calls from a pay phone.

PIERCE
(over his shoulder)

Everythin's in a company name. Don't go openin' any bank accounts…just pay your bills in cash. Lots of folks around here had eight hundred to spend…they'd think they were rich.

BILLY

What do you do for fun?

BUTLER

Movies, bowling, pool, country dancin'… watch TV, go to church.

PIERCE

You like to fish?

BILLY

Sure, that's the real reason I'm here.

PIERCE

I'll take you sometimes…got a boat.

They lapse into silence as the van speeds along the road next to the BAYOU.

TIME DISSOLVE

Van turns off paved road onto dirt road, bumps along a hundred feet or so, stops in front of a nicely-kept cabin, painted green and white, with a screened-porch.

They emerge, go into cabin.

INT. CABIN

Dark and cool. Heavy, old-fashioned wood furniture, some of the arms covered by lace antimacassars. Pegged wooden floors covered by old, but colorful, area rugs.

FOLLOW THEM into KITCHEN:

Right out of the thirties: free-standing Gaffers & Sattler half-propane, half-wood burning stove; porcelain Sears-Roebuck washing machine with hand wringer; a double sink, its white finish badly worn away, standing over exposed pipes. A linoleum-topped table and four wrought-iron chairs complete the room.

FOLLOW Billy through kitchen onto rear-screened porch.

HE EXITS to back yard, WALKS about thirty feet to end of grass, overlooking the bayou. HIS POV –

The bayou slopes sharply down and away from house, becoming a tangled mass of short MANGROVE trees sprouting from swampy land amid watery passages. Tall Eucalyptus and deciduous pines form a ceiling, broken only by small patches of blue sky. The mood in the bayou is DARK and spooky, even at noon.

ON BILLY

A look of uncertainty on his face. Listening to the alien sounds of the swamp, he shudders a little, turns and goes back in.

INT. CABIN

ON BILLY
As he enters.

                        PIERCE
Look here, whatever your name is. Big-screen TV. Did you see the satellite dish on the roof? Wasn't in our budget, but Butler's son-in-law sells them, got a deal.

                        BUTLER
Figure you're goin' be a little lonely way out here.

                        BILLY
What about transportation?

PIERCE
Pick-up's in the garage. Well, best be goin'.

BUTLER
Anythin' else you need? Fridge's stocked. Hope you like wieners and Bud…
(pointedly) We do.

PIERCE
One last thing. The local sheriff and highway patrol don't know about you. Best you keep out of their way. (offers business card and envelope) Don't call unless you know you're in danger. Here's your money. We'll be out to see you.

BUTLER
And stay away from the local women. Some of these hillbillies wouldn't think twice about feedin' you to the 'gators.

They EXIT, slamming the door behind them, get into their van and drive off, raising a cloud of dust.

BILLY - stares after them - a look of loneliness and apprehension on his face.

BEGIN FLASHBACK

INT. VINCE'S HOME OFFICE

SUPER: LEGEND ON SCREEN - "FOUR YEARS EARLIER"

ANGLE ON Vince, behind his desk; Billy stands in front.

VINCE
I'm sending you on a little paid vacation.

BILLY (light)
Could use one. Thanks for noticing. Hope it has a beach.

VINCE (ignores it)
I want you to fly down to Little Rock. A friend of mine named Smilin' Jack will meet you, drive you to Osceola. You'll pick up somethin' for me, bring it back here.

BILLY
Too big for Federal Express?

VINCE
You might say. It's a car.

BILLY
How come I'm going?

VINCE
Because you're my lawyer. You might have to do some fast talking.

BILLY
What's the deal?

VINCE
It's an old Ferrari, a 340S, one of a kind. Custom made in '54 for Batista. Raul Castro, that pimp, inherited it. He's a gambler, needs money. I bought it.

BILLY
So it's illegal from every standpoint…violates Trading With The Enemy statute, it's contraband. it's…

VINCE (cuts him off)
That's right, and it doesn't even have smog control. Here's what I want you to do.

CUT TO:

EXT. LITTLE ROCK INTERNATIONAL AIRPORT – DAY – STOCK

EASTERN Airlines 727 landing

INT. PASSENGER GATE

ANGLE - Billy coming through gate, being met by short, bald MAN in windbreaker. Big smile.

CUT TO:

INT. - CAR TRAVELING ALONG HIGHWAY

TWO-SHOT - Billy and Smilin' Jack.

JACK
It's on a private sugar shipper, buried under sacks of raw cane. They'll take it off tonight.

                    BILLY
It's drivable, isn't it? I've got over fifteen hundred miles to do.

                    JACK
Supposed to be in pretty good shape, but Ferraris, they're like women. You just never know. (smiles)

CUT TO: EXT. DESERTED DOCKS - LATE THAT NIGHT

CAMERA PANS UP At hoist, lowering a black Ferrari.

ANGLE ON Billy, Smilin' Jack and several SEAMEN, including the CAPTAIN.

HOIST - gently touches down. Seamen unstrap Ferrari; Billy and Jack both sign papers offered them by captain.

ON BILLY - Getting behind the wheel, turning key, grinning as engine catches, running roughly. Jack smiles back.

                    JACK (leans in window)
Back roads, remember. Use the map I gave you and drive at night. Obey the law, and be real nice to the cops if they wanna' look it over. They're all car nuts down here.

CUT TO:

EXT. HIGHWAY 91 - JUST AS IT ENTERS EL DORADO, ARKANSAS – NIGHT

INSIDE FERRARI - As Billy winds it down, turning into a side street just before the brightly lit main street begins. He parks, gets out, locks and starts walking into town.

FOLLOW HIM As he checks out the hunting and fishing stores, Dairy Queen, coffee shops, groceries, bowling alley, pool room, fast food palaces, movie triplex. Comes to a GAS STATION, walks in:

                    BILLY
                (to attendant)
Ran out of gas. Can I buy some? Need a can too.

                    ATTENDANT
Sure. I'll run you back after.

                    BILLY
Uh, no thanks. I don't mind walking.

Attendant gives him a funny look, fills 10-gallon gas can, accepts money, watches Billy walk away.

EXT. MC ALLISTER BRIDGE - between El Dorado and Shreveport –NIGHT

WIDE - Ferrari driving across.

ANGLE - Ferrari entering highway 55. HOLD on taillights disappearing in the distance.

INSIDE THE CAR

Billy drives, humming to himself. The Ferrari has no radio, and being a racer barely modified to the street, not much gauging, other than a speedometer calibrated in kilometers. The only light on this semi-rural road a few miles outside Shreveport is from the steadily dimming headlights, which continue to FADE.

ON BILLY - Wrinkles his nose, is something burning? He notices SMOKE coming from engine compartment.

BILLY
Fuck, I knew this would happen. Now what?

He speeds up, hoping to run into civilization before he runs out of time. PASSES an elderly DINER, various small, paint-peeled HOUSES, a USED TRUCK LOT, a tiny well-kept Black Baptist CHURCH, all closed.

THROUGH THE WINDSHIELD

Coming around a curve, a gas station sign: BOB'S FRIENDLY SINCLAIR SERVICE, a vintage one-hoist garage and two-pump gas station dating from just after World War II.

C.U. ON BILLY - He sighs relief, rolls in, shutting off the engine, pulling hand brake, SKIDDING to a stop near the pumps. He checks his watch.

INSERT - Still a few hours before dawn.

BACK ON HIM - As he pulls up his jacket collar and tries to get a little sleep.

EXT. GAS STATION - EARLY MORNING

A fairly new GMC "JIMMY" pulls in.

ON DRIVER dressed in MECHANIC'S OVERALLS notices the Ferrari, turns off his truck and APPROACHES. The MAN is tall, ruggedly handsome, in his early 40's. He has a shock of unruly black hair; a prominent, curved nose signals his Cajun lineage.

FROM INSIDE

Billy awakes with a start as mechanic knocks on the window. Billy rolls it down.

                        MECHANIC
          Got trouble? Didn't mean to scare ya'

                        BILLY
          Uh, yeah, fan belt broke, I think.

                        MECHANIC
          Let's take a look…gimme me a hand here.

Billy gets out. ON THEM AS They push the heavy racer onto the hoist. Ed pops the hood, looks down into engine.

                        MECHANIC
          Yeah, shredded. Gonna' be a problem getting you a replacement. No one around here's even seen one of these before. Probably take three-four days to get one.

                        BILLY
          What do you suggest? I don't have the time.

                        MECHANIC
          Could maybe fix you up. Let's see what I got.

TIME DISSOLVE

Billy walks around TOWN, checking it out as it awakens. He looks and feels a little out of place among the FARMERS, SHOPKEEPERS, and TRADESMEN.

BACK AT GARAGE - several hours LATER.

Billy watches mechanic put finishing touches on repair. Looks up at their reflection in plate glass window, sees something he didn't notice before:

WHAT HE SEES:

A RESEMBLANCE between himself and the other man; sharing similar shocks of unruly black hair, and largish, curved noses. That's it, but enough that from a distance, dressed similarly, they might be brothers.

                        MECHANIC
          There you go...start 'er up.

Billy gets behind wheel, starts engine. It runs cool.

> BILLY
> (relieved, smiles)
> How much do I owe you?

> MECHANIC
> Let's see. Charge you ten bucks for the air conditioning belt from that old Volkswagen, twenty more for my time. That OK?

> BILLY
> (takes out two 20's, hands it over)
> Here's forty. Worth it. What did you say your name was?

> MECHANIC
> Ed, Ed L'aborteaux…that's French. My great-grandfather. He fought in the Indian wars around here.

> BILLY
> Thanks, Ed. Don't imagine we'll ever see each other again, but you saved my life.

Ed nods as Billy drives off.

ON BILLY - Watching Ed's receding figure in the rear-view mirror. Can't help noticing, as Ed turns away, how much they look like each other, especially in profile.

END FLASHBACK:

EXT. DAY – PRESENT

CAMERA TRAVELS ROUTE 55, outside Shreveport.

PASSES the same elderly diner, this time with a few pick-ups and old sedans parked in front; same paint-peeling old houses, used truck lot, Black Baptist church. It is SUNDAY MORNING, and the CHOIR can be heard way down the road.

STOP at BOB'S FRIENDLY SINCLAIR SERVICE

POV FROM ACROSS THE ROAD

MED. – PUMPS

Ed pumps gas into a battered '69 Buick. Winding up, he wipes the windshield. An elderly BLACK WOMAN leans out.

                    WOMAN
          How much I owe you, Ed?

He peers at gauge.

INSERT - it reads $10.85

                    ED
          Ten dollars will do it, Alma

As she reaches toward her purse, a well-kept "Jimmy" pulls into station, stops behind Buick, engine idling.

INT. 'Jimmy'

Ed's wife, CINDY, a slim, pretty, blonde woman of 35, behind the wheel. Seated next to her, a gangly, 12-year old BOY, wearing a baseball cap, cradles two fishing poles in his lap.

EXT. SAME

Buick drives off; "Jimmy" pulls up to pumps. The boy jumps out.

                    BOY
          Ready, Dad?

                    ED
          Almost, T.J., just gonna' close up.

Ed leans into truck.

                    ED (cont.)
          Hello, gorgeous.

He kisses her, softly, but passionately.

                    CINDY
          Hi, yourself.

                    ED
          How was church?

                    CINDY (smiles)
          Very stimulating. You should try it sometime.

He pulls his head out, rests his hands on the truck door.

                    ED (mischievous look)
Honey, you know I gotta' work Sunday mornings. 'Ol Bob's too old! And, besides, if we want to buy this place someday, we need all we can put together.

                      CINDY
I know of several young unemployed men who'd be happy to spell you. And it wouldn't interfere with our plans. Bob's not about to sell to anyone but you.

                      ED
Perhaps so, hon'. T.J. and me'll see you for dinner, around five. Pray for fish!

He stands back as Cindy smiles ruefully, shakes her head and drives off with a wave.

CUT TO: EXT. 30-ft. walls of FEDERAL CORRECTIONAL CENTER, DANBURY –

DAY INT. VISITING ROOM - COME IN 0N Vince and his new son-in-law, Tony Greco, sitting opposite each other, behind bulletproof glass; speaking by telephone.

                      TONY
So, you feelin' any better, dad?

                      VINCE
I still got this pain, you know? The croakers here got no idea. Did you find me that specialist I asked you for?

                      TONY
Sure did. They're doin' the research now.

Vince nods, stands up heavily.

                      VINCE
How's my new granddaughter?

                      TONY
She's OK, but unfortunately, she looks like you.

Vince gives Tony an affectionate "fuck you" look, and LEAVES.

CUT TO:

The front of a new red and white MACK 350 Super Freightliner as it barrels down a highway, bearing down on CAMERA.

PAN UP THROUGH WINDSHIELD to I.D. OCCUPANTS of the cab.

C.U. – DRIVER CALVIN JACKSON, a good 'ol boy, mid-40's, wears a plaid shirt and a new straw cowboy hat, his stringy blond hair peeking out. He smokes a cheroot.

PAN TO CO-PILOT, Calvin's wife, JUDY, mid-30's, a good 'ol girl. Twin dark-brown pigtails frame her open, pretty but over-made up face. She wears her denim work shirt collar turned-up and unbuttoned to the third button.

INT. CAB

Judy pours from a thermos into plastic cup, offers it to Calvin.

> CALVIN
> Thanks, honey...where y'all want to eat tonite?

She consults unfolded map on her lap.

> JUDY
> Well...let's see. In Texarkana, they told us about "Clarkie's BBQ Fish Shack". That's about 30 miles down the road, just outside Shreveport. Be there before dark.

> CALVIN
> Barbequed Fish? What's up with these yuppie hillbillies? First they burned it, called it cajun, now they're sloppin' sauce on it. I don't know...that whatcha' want?

ON HER - she nods, smiles at him. He smiles back, stomps on the accelerator.

POV THROUGH THE WINDSHIELD as the Sun sinks toward the horizon, signs flash by. The Mack 350 is on highway 55.

CUT TO:

EXT. CLARKIE's BBQ FISH SHACK - THAT EVENING

The Mack rolls in to the parking area and shuts down, its air brakes and suspension sighing like a weary dragon. ANGLE ON Calvin and Judy as they get down from their high perch and walk stiffly toward the neon-lit restaurant front.

INT. A family place, piney wood walls, red-checkered tablecloths, napkin dispensers and Louisiana hot sauce on the tables, which appear to be all taken.

HOSTESS

Hi. y'all, just two tonight?

JUDY

Yes, mam', and we're real hungry. That right, Calvin?

CALVIN
(licks his lips)

Hm..hm...can't wait.

HOSTESS

This way, please.

FOLLOW AS she leads them to a table near the kitchen, they sit. Hostess leaves them.

CALVIN
(to Judy)

Wonder, can ya' get a beer here?

An elderly waitress, her hair in a long out-of-fashion bee-hive, appears.

WAITRESS

I heard that...and you surely can. Miller or Bud?

CALVIN

That all? Nothin' imported?

JUDY
(to Calvin, then waitress)

Oh, hush...mam', he'll have a Bud...make that two.

WAITRESS
(having fun)

I'll have to see some ID for you, mam'. Don't need to worry about that old goat there.

CALVIN
(mock offense)

Hold on, there, I want to see some ID on you...darn kids they hire these days to wait on folks.

WAITRESS
(smiles, made her point)

Be right back with your drinks. We serve what's on the blackboard there.

They crane their necks to see what's on the menu above the small bar.

                JUDY
Oh look, baby. Smothered catfish, your favorite. And barbequed eel...and crayfish..

                CALVIN
            (wrinkles his nose)
Ugh...those are just big insects...too hard to eat anyway.

               WAITRESS
           (putting down beers)
Special tonight's Chicken-fried Pompano...recommend it.

They look at each other, make a decision.

                CALVIN
Sold. And while we gotcha', tell me, where do the livelies go to country dance 'round here?

               WAITRESS
      (lowers her voice, looks around)
You mean white folks, don'tcha..

                CALVIN
Well, uh, yeah.

               WAITRESS
              (relieved)
That'd be Belle's Dance Hall, in Stevenville - not far. Let me get your order in.

DISSOLVE - COME UP ON Calvin and Judy finished with dinner. He picks his teeth while she searches out her money. MAN approaches.

                 MAN
Howdy, folks, I'm Tommy Clark. I haven't seen you in here before. Everythin' to your liking?

                CALVIN
           (stretches out his hand)
Hell yes, Tommy. Real good. Don't think I've ever had anythin' just like it.

                JUDY
Enjoyed it. We just started pushing our rig up from New Orleans to Little Rock, and back.

TOMMY
Real good...hope to see ya' again.

CALVIN
Sure will. Hey, Tommy, before you go, help us out with a few things?

TOMMY
Surely, if I can.

CALVIN
You got to be a fisherman, where do you go around here, you know, personally?

TOMMY
I can't give that away, but if you gonna be by this way Sunday mornin', you come along with me, I guarantee you some fish.

CALVIN
Don't know if we can, but we'll try.

JUDY
Oh, Tommy, one last question. Know a good mechanic for our truck? Never near a dealer when we need one, and we always like to keep a list of the good locals.

TOMMY
Well, let's see. There's Addis Bronnick. He's a truck man, over there in Emeryville. And, (thinks a moment) I don't know if he's up on your kind of rig, but Ed L'aborteaux can fix any motor I ever heard of.

JUDY
Ed L'aborteaux? How do you spell that... and where is he, exactly?

TOMMY
Here, lend me your pen, I'll write it out for you.

As he does, Calvin and Judy exchange bland looks.

JUDY
(looking down at napkin)
Why, thank you, you're mighty kind.

TOMMY
Not a'tall. See you Sunday, I hope.

As he walks away, Calvin and Judy push away from table and head for the door.

CUT TO:

EXT. TRAVELING HIGHWAY 55 – NIGHT- SOUNDS OF Crickets, Bullfrogs, Katydids. The landscape is mostly dark. Here and there, low lights in closed stores flash by. Not much traffic.

IN THE DISTANCE - A CLOSED FILLING STATION.

As CAMERA approaches, the sign reads "Bob's Friendly Sinclair Service." SLOW DOWN as it passes station –

POV - MECHANIC'S BAY lit by single light. Someone is still working.

ANGLE ON

Ed L'aborteaux, putting an ancient Evinrude outboard motor back together.

HE LOOKS UP As a bright, shiny new Mack 350 Freightliner, red and white, rolls slowly by.

                         ED
               (to himself, a low whistle)
That's a beauty...wonder what livin' on the road like that would be. Nah, Cindy wouldn't give up her kitchen.

He smiles to himself, shakes his head, and returns to his work.

CUT TO:

INT. MACK CAB - LOOKING OUT AT THE ROAD

                        JUDY
    Just around that bend.

ON CALVIN As he applies the air brakes, slowly bringing the monster truck to a STOP.

ON JUDY As she turns around, perching on her knees, reaches behind the seat for a small black CASE.

                      CALVIN
    Hang on a sec'. We can't be that lucky.

                                JUDY
                Lucky? We've been on this job for two months. How much more catfish can you
                eat?

Reaching into the glove compartment, Calvin pulls out an envelope. Opening it, he stares at a photograph.

INSERT: It's a picture of Billy, taken at a party several years ago. He looks a little drunk.

                                CALVIN
                Here, take it with you. Don't screw up, make sure it's him.

POV FROM THE ROAD:

As Judy jumps out, Calvin puts the Mack into gear and slowly drives off.

BACK ON JUDY:

Bending low, disappears into the roadside foliage.

CUT TO: INT. GARAGE:

Ed is winding up his repairs for the night - putting the head cover back on the motor. He yawns, covering his mouth with his hand, leaving a black, greasy smear.

CUT TO:

Silently as possible, Judy arrives in the heavy brush opposite the garage. Taking a mini-maglite with a red lens from her pocket and holding it between her teeth, she opens the case.

INSERT:

A Browning Target Match .22 caliber, single shot rifle, Mark 3 silencer and 10X50 telescopic sight, broken down and resting securely in foam.

BACK ON HER:

Working quickly and silently, she assembles the rifle, inserting a Long Rifle Magnum Hollow Point bullet.

INSERT: THROUGH the lens of the SCOPE we SEE Ed in the CROSSHAIRS.

ON JUDY'S TENSE FACE - Snuggled against the rifle stock.

ANGLE - She quickly looks down at the photo, searching for the resemblance.

>   JUDY
>   (to herself - V.O.)
>   It's him...goddam it. Same hair...same nose.

INSERT: Her trigger finger TIGHTENING.

CUT BACK TO ED –

Fumbles a small screw, reaches for it, DROPS his head slightly to search in the shadows.

THROUGH THE TELESCOPIC SIGHT AGAIN: Image ROCKS slightly from the muffled gunpowder explosion.

SMASH CUT:

Ed JUMPS aside as the 150-grain bullet SHATTERS into a thousand pieces of tiny shrapnel against the rusting corrugated steel siding behind him.

>   ED
>   (to himself)
>   Shit! That was close! Damn kids foolin' around. Probably a mile away...didn't even
>   hear the shot.

ACROSS THE ROAD:

A grim Judy, carrying her rifle and case, keeping low against the tree line, dashes back through the brush.

HER POV: Around a bend, the Mack waits. She races toward it.

DISSOLVE OUT AND IN:

INT. DARKENED ROOM- EARLY MORNING

In bed, a figure sleeps. CAMERA PANS - tattered old blankets tacked against the windows keep out the growing light. The figure tosses restlessly.

SOUNDS OF SLOW, HEAVY FOOTSTEPS

In the kitchen startle the sleeping figure, which SITS UP abruptly.

ON BILLY: He freezes, and listens. The footsteps come closer.

ANGLE ON Billy, quietly getting out of bed, stealing behind door where he picks up a baseball bat.

> BILLY
> (to himself)
> Bastards...how did they find me so fast...? That cocksucker Drago...they got to him.. must've tipped 'em off.

Something THUDS against the door. Billy jumps a foot, terrified.

Another BUMP - Summoning up his courage and hoping to talk his way out of a bullet, Billy grabs the door handle, flinging OPEN the door and sees - An ALLIGATOR, six feet long, three feet of which is jaws and teeth, grinning up at him. Billy slams the door shut, slides to the floor, wet with sweat.

CUT TO:

EXT. SPIDER LAKE - EARLY MORNING –

Before sun-up. In the gray dawn, a single rowboat silhouetted on the still water. Hunched over, staying warm, a lone FISHERMAN, his line motionless, waits for the fish to awaken. The only SOUNDS - tiny waves lapping against the boat, and a gentle wind. It's too early even for the birds.

TRAVEL ACROSS the water to BOAT

MED. C.U. Ed, the fisherman, quietly pours himself a hot coffee from his thermos, blows on it, sips.

ANGLE ON HILLS: Getting lighter with the rising sun.

BACK TO ED –

Decides to pull in his line, change his bait. Cocks his head: hears something unusual; a deep RUMBLING SOUND. He looks up, but doesn't see anything. Changing lures, he STANDS up to cast. The noise grows LOUDER as his Bass Master Lunker lands precisely among the reeds and cattails near shore.

ON ED As he looks curiously to the source of the growing racket.

HIS POV: From around a small cape, the menacing prow of a massive CIGARETTE 210 speedboat emerges and slowly travels across the horizon. A single FARAWAY FIGURE pilots it.

> ED
> (to himself)
> Whew...a Cigarette. Man, what a boat…Wait'll I tell T.J. what he missed by sleepin' in. Wonder who owns that monster?

ANGLE ON CIGARETTE:

Picking up SPEED, begins to describe a long ARC in Ed's direction.

>   ED
>   (watching carefully)
> Hope that dumb sonofoabitch doesn't head this way...gonna' ruin my fishin' sure... he's got the whole damned lake to play in.

BACK ON CIGARETTE: Heading right at CAMERA, its 400HP engine roaring like an F-15 jet in full thrust.

C.U. ON ED

>   ED
>   (puts his pole down, waves his arms, yells)
> Hey, hey....you're headin' right at me... Turn...turn!

ED'S POV –

Knife-edge of the Cigarette's prow BEARING DOWN on him at 75 mph. Just visible above the prow, the DRIVER wears a SKI MASK.

SECONDS LATER: Just before impact, Ed dives into the lake, quickly submerging as the Cigarette SMASHES through the rowboat, shattering it.

ON THE WRECKAGE:

Ed's eyes cautiously rise above the turbulent water. He takes care to stay hidden behind a largish piece of debris.

IN THE DISTANCE –

The killer boat makes a wide turn and heads back toward him, slower this time.

MONTAGE: As the Cigarette, hunting, grids across the wreckage-strewn, now still waters.

WATCH ED: Alternately hiding and submerging, avoiding discovery, until eventually, the masked driver speeds away.

CUT TO:

INT. SHERIFF'S OFFICE - LATER THAT MORNING

ANGLE ON Ed and SHERIFF BUSTER RAINES

                    ED
Only time I ever been that scared was that night when you and I got caught all alone on that hill by that 'Cong patrol. No radio, no flares, nearly no ammo.

                    BUSTER
                (burly, bearded)
Yeah, well, they weren't no turkey hunters like us. They knew we were there, but never could find us.

He stands, walks with a pronounced limp to coffeemaker, pours two cups, returns to desk, sits, pushing one cup to Ed.

                    BUSTER (cont.)
Weren't for that mine, woulda' had two legs today. Hell, got me home earlier than you, else you woulda' been sheriff, and Id'a been the grease monkey.

                    ED
Buster, somebody's out to kill me, and I can't figure out the who and why.

                    BUSTER
Looks that way. That bullet the other night was meant for you. Just lucky they missed.

Ed stands, paces.

                    ED
Who could it be? No enemies I know of. Grew up right here, know the same folks you do. Only time we ever left was when we joined up to go to 'Nam.

                    BUSTER
                (chuckles)
Some of them farmers whose sons you coach in Little League sure hate your guts sometimes.

                    ED
                (shaking off the humor)
Hey, Buster, you think maybe it's about 'Nam?

                    BUSTER
Could be. Lot of Vietnamese fisherman been settlin' all along the Gulf, mainly Texas and Louisiana. Rubbin' the locals the wrong way, been bump-ups, torn nets, even shootouts.

                              ED
          God, Buster, that was over 20 years ago. Who the hell did I piss off?

                              BUSTER
          Who didn't we? You might remember we were LURPs, long-range patrol, Special
          Forces. On our own, out of contact for months at a time. We lived off the land and
          the peasants, and we had to be damned sure who we were talking to.

                              ED
          You think that's maybe it?

Buster limps over to coffee pot for a refill.

                              BUSTER
          Don't know. There's a lot of loonies running around down here in the sticks these
          days. Big city types running away from crime, bringin' their problems with them,
          drug dealers hiding out, even some gangsters in the witness protection program.
          Hell, the feds don't even tell us who they are.

                              ED
          I get it...those are pretty much the only people who could afford a boat like that.

                              BUSTER
          Don't know what to tell 'ya. Be careful, is all. You gonna' talk to your wife and son '
          bout this?

                              ED
          Not yet. Don't want them worryin'. Seems like whoever they are just want me.

On Ed's concerned look:

CUT TO:

EXT. - Bob's Friendly Sinclair Service - DAY

SUPER LEGEND ONSCREEN: A MONTH LATER

ANGLE ON Ed making change for the school bus DRIVER, an ELDERLY LADY, handing it up through the window.

ANOTHER ANGLE - The red and white Mack 350 Freightliner cruises slowly by.

ON ED - Glances at it another time.

> BUS DRIVER
> (following his look)
> Sure is a beauty. Seems to be a regular 'round here.

CUT TO:

EXT. L'ABORTEAUX HOME – DAY

ANGLE ON CINDY, holding an envelope, walking to the road. She waits.

ANOTHER ANGLE - DOWN THE ROAD - U.S. MAIL RURAL DELIVERY PICK-UP TRUCK STOPS. She leans in.

> CINDY
> 'Morning, Arthur.

> MAILMAN

'Morning, Cindy. Here's your mail. What's that you got?

> CINDY

Certified letter to the school board. Could you post it for me? Save me a trip to town.

> MAILMAN

Sure. T.J. actin' up again?

> CINDY

'Fraid so. They're talkin' suspension.

> MAILMAN

'Bout to be a teenager. Better hang on.

She waves as the truck pulls away. FOLLOW HER - Returning up path to house, examining mail.

INT. KITCHEN

CINDY puts usual collection of bills, hunting and fishing magazines down, takes Reader's Digest for herself, looks closely at brown paper-wrapped package.

INSERT: Ordinary brown paper-wrapped package marked "Fishing Lures"

MED. SHOT:

                    CINDY
                  (to herself)
        That man...if he couldn't fish. Such a sucker.

She puts it down on shelf next to refrigerator, where she knows Ed will go first for a cold beer when he gets home.

CUT TO: KITCHEN DOOR –

SLAMS as T.J. and his GERMAN SHEPHERD STORM IN.

T.J. goes right to refrigerator for a Dr. Pepper. He notices package, picks it up, shakes it, puts it down carelessly, half-on, half-off counter.

PHONE in OTHER ROOM RINGS.

T.J. dashes off to get it.

                    T.J.
        It's for me....

The Shepherd, in his haste to follow, leaps after T.J., and knocks the package to the floor, where - With a DEAFENING ROAR, it EXPLODES!

DISSOLVE OUT AND IN - INT. SHATTERED KITCHEN – LATER

ANGLE ON Ed, Buster and his deputy ALEX survey the damage.

                    ED
        I'm goin' underground, Buster. Time I started fightin' back. Appreciate your keepin' an eye on my family.

                    BUSTER
        Yeah, think you should, for a while. Give us a chance to figure out what's happenin'. Where will you be?

                    ED
        'Round the caves. Bears keep most deer hunters n' tourists away.

ON BUSTER AND ALEX - Buster nods.

CUT TO:

EXT. L'ABORTEAUX HOUSE - THAT NIGHT

ANGLE ON Ed, his face darkened, wearing camouflage gear, and a backpack, carries a rifle and crossbow. He steals quietly across the yard and disappears into the trees.

CUT TO:

EXT. MAIN STREET - EL DORADO, ARKANSAS – DAY

ANGLE ON Billy, sitting at a booth in the "Pick-Me-Up" luncheonette; done with his breakfast, he drinks a cup of coffee while reading the local NEWS-PRESS. He spots a story of interest to him, brings the paper closer.

INSERT: HEADLINE - "MAIL BOMB EXPLODES IN LOCAL MECHANIC'S HOME"- SUB-HEAD - "Woman and 12-year old son uninjured. Husband disappears" - accompanied by a graphic b&w PHOTO of the destroyed kitchen.

C.U. BILLY - Frowns as he reads the part about the missing mechanic.

ANGLE ON WAITRESS LOLA, a cute teenager, kinky red hair in two long braids down her back, appears behind him, coffee pot in hand, looks over his shoulder:

>   WAITRESS
> Oh, Lord, heard about that on the radio. Communists, most likely. Ain't nobody safe no more.

>   BILLY
>   (looks up, smiles)
> Communists, where'd you hear that? There's no communists anymore, Lola.

>   LOLA
> Sure is, Ed. Right here in America is where all them Reds is hidin'. Heard it from Jimmy Swaggart on TV, and anything he says is true.

Billy shakes his head, motions for more coffee.

CUT TO:

INT. DANBURY CORRECTIONAL PRISON – DAY

ANGLE ON Vince and Tony, again talking by phone on opposite sides of the glass.

>   VINCE
> I'm gettin' sicker by the minute, Tony.

>   TONY
> I can see that, Vince. What do you want me to do?

> VINCE
> Fire those doctors. They're amateurs. I want another specialist, someone I can trust.

> TONY
> OK, Vince, I'll handle it. Any suggestions?

> VINCE
> Yeah, I want you to take personal charge of this. You understand?

> TONY
> (apprehensive, but honored)
> Sure...sure I do.

> VINCE
> The problem is very obvious. I don't understand why they just can't see it, know what I'm sayin'?

Tony nods.

> VINCE
> But you gotta' be careful, 'cause people will be lookin' over your shoulder… professional jealousy, right?

Vince looks keenly at Tony, who knows this is his big chance to inherit.

> VINCE (cont.)
> So my kid's pregnant again...that all you do.\?

> TONY (grins)
> Yeah, matter of fact...we're gonna' have a dozen by the time you get out.

> VINCE
> Get outta' here, punk. Let me know when I can expect to feel better.

CUT TO:

INT. KERR'S SPORTING GOODS - BOSTON – DAY

MONTAGE: Tony trying on hunting clothes; in GUN ROOM, sighting down a REMINGTON.270 Magnum Sporter, semi-automatic, with 10-power scope.

MED: On Tony at gun counter with salesman.

                              SALESMAN
    These are "Black Talons", 170-grain hollow points that burst into six claws. Rips
    right through your animal, kills it quicker.

                              TONY
                        (smiles, examines box)
    You read my mind.

CUT TO:

INT. AVIS CAR RENTAL OFFICE - SHREVEPORT – DAY

ANGLE ON DESK: Tony and two "associates," SAL and ITSY. The three, dressed in brand-new, up-scale hunting attire, carrying new rifle cases look exactly like the tourists they're supposed to be.

CLERK hands Tony keys and the three exit through back door towards parking area.

CUT TO:

SAME STRETCH OF HIGHWAY 55 – WIDE

JEEP CHEROKEE containing Tony, Sal and Itsy pulls into Bob's Friendly Sinclair Station.

ANGLE ON ATTENDANT - Coming out to meet them; MYRON, a tall, gangly, acned, blonde kid of about 17.

FROM INSIDE JEEP

                              TONY
    Fill 'er up.

Myron hooks up, starts washing windshield.

                              TONY
                        (leans out, to Myron)
    Good huntin' around here?

                              MYRON
    Real good, if you know where to look.

                              TONY
    We could use a guide. Know anyone?

Myron finishes window, looks in.

85

MYRON
(trying for nonchalance)
Well, season's on, most guides are busy. Only one left I know about...happens to be the best.

TONY
How much for the best?

MYRON
Uh, hundred a day...each? Guarantee you your limit.

TONY
You know these woods, huh?

MYRON
Like my face, mister. I'm a tracker.

TONY
(looking in his rear-view at Sal)
OK, kid, you got a deal. We're at the Holiday Inn.

MYRON
(excited)
Alright! Pick y'all up at five am.

INT. JEEP: Itsy groans.

TONY
More money than this kid's ever seen. He's gonna' take us just where we want to go.

CUT TO:

INT. POOLROOM – NIGHT - Smokey - Blue-collar crowd.

ANGLE ON Myron, holding a stick, drinking a beer, watching his friend DON play.

DON
Three bills a day. That's more than cranky ol' Bob pays you in a month. Enough to keep your daddy drunk and in venison all year. Better try and stretch it out.

MYRON
Chinese fella's at the restaurant down the road pay real good for bear gall bladder. Say it makes their peckers hard. (which makes them giggle.

CUT TO:

EXT. THE WOODS - EARLY MORNING

CAMERA PANS - dappled sunlight slowly lighting up deep shadows. Slight WIND stirs branches. Nothing seems to be moving - until -

ANGLE - From behind a small hill, a camouflaged FIGURE moves toward a rocky outcropping.

CAMERA ZOOMS IN to I.D. ED. FOLLOW HIM as he cautiously investigates entrance to a CAVE. Picks up a rock, knocks it LOUDLY on cave entrance; waits a moment, throws rock into cave. SOUNDS of rock bouncing off walls. Satisfied, he enters.

INT. CAVE - SAME - LIT by his flashlight, Ed looks around; barely big enough for him to stand. PAN CAVE - Reaches back some fifteen feet, sloping to floor. Checking SIGN, Ed focuses on SCAT.

                    ED
                (to himself)
Hasn't been used since last winter - got a couple of weeks at least before hibernation.

Gets busy setting up CAMP.

CUT TO:

EXT. BILLY'S CABIN - DAY

Billy emerges with small suitcase, goes to pick-up, throws case on seat, gets in and drives away.

INT. PICK-UP - SAME - He fiddles with radio, trying for anything but country-western and Baptist bible-thumpers. No luck. Disgusted, he stabs the off button.

EXT. MAIN STREET - EL DORADO - SAME –

ON BILLY'S TRUCK as it parks. Billy exits, walks down street until he reaches a SCAGGS Drug Store. Enters.

INT. SCAGGS - SAME - Billy and CLERK at rear gun counter. Billy is examining automatic pistols. Clerk picks one up, fondles it

                    CLERK
I can sell you this Desert Eagle, made in Israel...50 caliber, biggest handgun there is...you probably seen Stallone and Schwarzenegger use it in the movies. But if you're goin' deer huntin', this one's the best. (picks up a machine pistol) MAC-DG 10 nine-millimeter semi-auto. Holds 17, but I can sell you a 30-shot banana clip. (leans in, lowers his voice) Got a gunsmith friend who'll hellfire your trigger, if you like.

                        BILLY
            Make it automatic, you mean? Take long?

                        CLERK
            While you wait. I'll just phone him up.

CUT TO:

EXT. BILLY'S TRUCK - LATER - As he climbs in, putting paper-wrapped box and stuffed backpack on seat next to him. Starts up, drives off.

CUT TO:

EXT. - MC ALLISTER BRIDGE - SAME - HELI. SHOT - BILLY'S PICK-UP CROSSING BRIDGE

BACK INSIDE CAB - BILLY'S POV

                        BILLY
                    (to himself)
            Vince's fucked it up! I gotta' do this hit myself, then I call Drago, get a new
            name…and I'm free.

He turns onto highway 55, joining flow of traffic.

CUT TO:

INT. CAVE - EARLY MORNING - Filtered light. ON ED - SLEEPING. On platform he's formed from pine boughs, his folded jacket his pillow. The remains of a small fire still smolder in front of his face.

C.U. - HE HEARS SOMETHING - Sits up, takes his binocs and rifle, quietly moves to cave opening.

HIS POV THRU GLASSES - Across the next hill, half a mile away, FOUR FIGURES in the dawn light move below the ridge top so as not to be silhouettes. Watching a moment more, he lowers the binocs.

                        ED
                    (to himself)
            Myron, that dipshit, and some tourists. At least they're not headed this way.

CUT TO:

EXT. BOB'S FRIENDLY SINCLAIR SERVICE - DAY

Billy gets out his truck, as OL' BOB himself, totters out to service him. Bob is in his eighties, bent over with age, and true to his rep, cranky. Probably because his teeth don't fit too well.

                    OL' BOB
          Howdy...fill 'er up?

                    BILLY
          Yeah.

Ol' Bob can hardly get around, so after putting the pump into the truck's filler neck, he hands Billy a couple of paper towels and points to a pail of water with a squeegee sticking out.

                    OL' BOB
          Hep' yerself.

                    BILLY
          No need, thanks. Run this place by yourself?

                    OL' BOB
          Can't get good hep' these days. Willin' to go's high as four bucks an hour too. Used to be, we had a work ethic in this country...that's how come we beat the Japs.

                    BILLY
          I was through here a couple years back. You had a pretty good mechanic then...tall, black hair, kinda' large nose.

                    OL' BOB
          Oh, hell, you mean Ed. I was gonna' sell out to him when I got old enough. Changed my mind, though. Had some problems, so he just up and disappeared into the bayous. T'were me, I would'a stood up. Snotnose kid I hired to replace him's gone too.

                    BILLY
          Mind if I use your telephone?

                    OL' BOB
          Payphone's all there is.

FOLLOW BILLY TO SIDE OF STATION - He picks up dangling phone book, quickly thumbs through, finds what he's looking for, returns to truck. Ol' Bob squints at meter.

                    OL' BOB
          Didn't take a whole lot.

Billy pays, gets in truck and drives off.

EXT. RESIDENTIAL STREET - SAME - FOLLOW BILLY'S TRUCK As it cruises slowly down street.

INT. TRUCK - ON BILLY - Looking for numbers - continues driving.

POV THRU TRUCK WINDOW - Billy sees a group of young kids returning from school - among them, T.J.

EXT. STREET

Billy's truck rounds corner. BACK INSIDE TRUCK - Billy cranks the wheel, makes a U-turn, stops at corner. HE SEES T.J. enter driveway. Billy starts out into intersection, turns, passes L'aborteaux house as T.J. goes in.

CUT TO:

EXT. EARLY MORNING - NEXT DAY

Billy's truck rounds corner just as T.J. leaves house for school. FOLLOW TRUCK - As it pulls up next to T.J.

                        BILLY (calls out)
Excuse me, young man.

                        T.J.
Me? (looks around)

                        BILLY
Can you help me...I'm from across the river, and I'm lost.

STOPS TRUCK - Billy leans over, opens door. T.J. comes over.

                        BILLY
                 (holds piece of paper)
You know the L'aborteaux family?

                        T.J.
                 (leans in, looks at paper)

Well, yeah, sure. That's my family.

                        BILLY
Good, get in.

                    T.J. (starts to back away)
            Get in? Why, who are you?

T.J.'S POV - Billy uncovers the MAC-10 DG machine pistol in his hand.

                    BILLY
            I've got your dad. If you ever want to see him again, you better get in.

ON T.J., SCARED - Hesitates, then gets in.

EXT. REAR OF TRUCK as it drives away.

CUT TO:

EXT. DEEP INSIDE THE BAYOU - LATER

DARK, steamy with humidity - strange SOUNDS and MOVEMENT.

ANGLE ON Billy and T.J. making their way through the SWAMP. T.J. wears a DOG COLLAR, padlocked at his throat, attached to a retracting lead. Billy, wearing the heavy backpack, holds the lead's handle and stays about ten feet behind

                    T.J.
            You're the guy that tried to kill us with that bomb, right? What did my dad ever do to you?

                    BILLY
                    (sweating, brushing insects off his face)
            I told you, kid, I don't know anything about any bomb. Its business, I just want to talk to him.

                    T.J.
            Yeah, I'm sure...with a gun.

ON BILLY - As he SLIPS on wet mud, skids down a small hill to the water's edge, dragging T.J. off his feet and down with him.

                    BILLY
            Oof! Godammit...

Billy gets up painfully. He's scraped his arm; his pants at his knee are torn, and BLOOD seeps through. Just then, a WATER MOCASSIN shoots across their path and into the water.

                    BILLY
          (alarmed, he jumps, yanking T.J.)
     Shit! Watch out...a snake!

                    T.J. (grins)
     They ain't poisonous.

Billy glares at him.

                    BILLY
     C'mon...let's get goin'!

T.J. leads them up a STEEP hill. Billy, gritting his teeth through his growing exhaustion, painfully follows.

CUT TO:

EXT. SWAMP - LATER

ON ED: Patrolling his area. He moves silently, crossbow strapped across his chest, keeping himself nearly invisible by darting low from tree to tree. Noticing something, he squints at small tree branch:

INSERT - Broken and twisted, just so.

C.U. ED - Thoughtful as he rolls the twist between his fingers.

                    ED
          (to himself...annoyed)
     T.J.? What's he doing...I told him to stay home, take care of his mom.

Ed continues his patrol, disappearing into the shadows.

EXT. FOREST FLOOR - MID-MORNING

ANGLE ON Myron, Tony, Itsy and Sal noisily making their way through dense THICKETS, flushing rabbits and ground birds. It's HOT, and they're sweating.

Myron, ten yards ahead, slips easily through the brush, but the city slickers, shouldering backpacks, trip over roots and rocks, run into overhanging branches, muttering curses, brushing clouds of late-hatching MAYFLIES from their faces.

                    MYRON
          (turns around, speaks low)
     Shhhh...them whitetails can hear ya' a mile.

Tony gives him a disgusted look.

                        ITSY
      (stops a minute, peels off his jacket, mops his face - to Tony)
What are we gonna' do if we actually see a deer...I ain't gonna' shoot some poor dumb animal.

                        SAL
Me neither, we got pets at home.

                        TONY
I can't understand you guys…you got no problem wastin' bozos, but just because you saw "Bambi" when you were kids....Shit, well, one of us better take a shot or he'll catch on…just aim high.

CUT TO:

EXT. THE FOREST - ON A HILL - ANGLE FROM BEHIND ED - Glassing the area.

THROUGH THE BINOC LENS - SWAYING BRANCHES, something moving through. PAN UP TO CANOPY - BIRDS, disturbed, rise from their perches, attempting to draw the threat away from their nests.

ED stows his binocs, starts DOWN the hill to investigate. FOLLOW HIM as he tracks, silent and unseen, through the haunting bayous.

CUT TO:

EXT. FOREST - HIGH GROUND NEAR THE BEAR CAVES.

Myron leads Tony, Itsy and Sal to the rock cliffs where Ed has his base camp. STOPS to listen:

                        MYRON
      (looks up at Sun high overhead)
Too hot to hunt now. We'll set up in a cave and wait for dusk, when they come out to feed.

                        ITSY
Sounds good to me. Who's got the booze?

MONTAGE: They select a cave, unload, slide to the ground, exhausted by their hard climb.

CUT TO:

EXT. FOREST - DUSK

SONGS of the day birds have stopped; SOUNDS of the night animals echo spookily through the black trees. CAMERA PANS - In the DISTANCE, the light of a small fire;

FROM BEHIND ED - As he cautiously and silently approaches the firelight. HE SEES his SON, captive to a strange man.

ZOOM IN on padlocked dog collar around T.J.'s neck.

MED. SHOT

T.J. feeds dead branches into the fire, while Billy, squatting on his haunches, machine pistol across his knees, roots through his backpack for dinner.

                    ED
                (to himself)
    Damn...he's usin' T.J. as bait...

He writhes with anger as he watches Billy YANK T.J. down beside him. Although Ed can't make out the words, Billy's anger is obvious.

                ED (cont.)
    Gotta' have a plan...too dangerous to do anythin' now. He's a brave kid...be alright 'till mornin'.

Ed quietly leaves the area.

CUT TO:

EXT. FOREST - NIGHT

By AVAILABLE LIGHT - the sheer rock face of the cave wall ghostly shimmers in the distance. FOLLOW ED as he slips through the trees, approaching his base. He STOPS... listens: On the WIND, the murmur of VOICES: WATCH HIM make a wide half-circle around the strangers.

HIS POV THROUGH THE TREES

                ED (sotto voce)
    Oh no, that little prick Myron, and his tourists again! Might've figured he'd come here. At least I can do something about this.

ANGLE ON GROUP

Tony, Sal & Itsy sit on ground around the campfire, leaning back on fallen logs, DRINKING pretty steadily. Myron fries rabbit he's killed for dinner, with wild onion. It SMELLS pretty good.

SUDDENLY, A RUSTLING IN THE TREES.

ON ED - Cradling his rifle, his dark, scowling, half-Indian countenance shadowed by the firelight, steps out into the open. MYRON JUMPS up in fear. He never heard a sound. PAN TO INCLUDE Tony, Sal & Itsy, drunk as they are, reach for their rifles and stumble to a standing position.

>   ED
> Easy, folks, nothing to fear.
>
>   MYRON
>   (sheepish)
> It's OK, I know him...he's my coach.
>
>   TONY
> What the hell did you major in…sneakin' around?
>
>   ED
> Need to be quiet so you don't scare the game.
>
>   MYRON
> How's your luck?
>
>   ED
> S'what I came to say...I've pretty much hunted out this area. Haven't seen a buck legal to take. (squats by the fire) So we don't get in each other's way, I suggest you all hunt the pine meadows over yonder by the creek. I'll be goin' up into the aspens, see if they've still got enough water to hide out for awhile.

They relax, put down their weapons, collapse back down to a seated position. The firelight, flickering up, outlines their features.

>   MYRON
> Could let ya' have some rabbit if you're hungry.
>
>   ED
> No, thanks.
>
>   TONY
>   (holds out flask)
> You a bourbon man?

                    ED
                (takes it)
        I don't mind. Thanks.

He takes a solid drink, returns it to Tony, stands.

                    ED
        Well, best be gettin' to bed. Good huntin'.

And disappears into the woods.

                    TONY
        Who'd you say that was?

                    MYRON
        Oh, coach? Ed. He runs the garage where I work. Used to, anyway.

                    SAL
        How do you mean?

                    MYRON
                (serving up rabbit)
        He's runnin'. Somebody tried to kill him. Almost got his family.

                    ITSY
                (sneers)
        In this hick town?

                    SAL
        Sure. This is America, there's violence everywhere. Don't you watch TV?

                    TONY
        Wait a minute. Listen, kid, what's the story? Was he back-dooring some other guy's wife?

                    MYRON
        Heck, no. Ed' a square. Nobody can figure it out. Sheriff's stumped.

                    TONY
        What's his last name?

                    MYRON
        L'aborteaux - French-Indian...family's been here 200 years.

Tony looks at Sal & Itsy. They got it!

TONY
Listen, kid. I know you know what you're doin', but we're payin', so we're gonna' change the plan a little, OK?

MYRON
Uh, sure. Um...I'm sorry we didn't get a deer today...but..

SAL
Shut up and listen, kid.

TONY
I have a feeling your coach knows just where to hunt. So we're gonna' stay on his tail, only he's not gonna' know it. Think you can handle that?

MYRON
(looking glum)
Yeah.

TONY
Let's turn in. (to Sal & Itsy) Take a walk with me. I gotta' pee.

They walk a little distance away.

TONY (sotto voce)
No wonder he scammed Pauli and Deb, the prick! He's usin' this local yokel's name. Fuckin' good thing I'm here to figure it out.

SAL
Fuck you, Tony. They're the best there is and you know it.

TONY
Posin' as shit-kickin' truckers...I sent them on a job, Sally, not to audition for some cowboy movie.

SAL
Hang on, Tone, you're not still hung up on Debbie, are you? You two nearly killed each other.

ITSY
You should kiss Pauli's ass for takin' her outta' your life.

TONY
(softening)
I think about her sometimes. Toughest and sweetest woman I ever met. Never knew which side I'd see.

                              SAL
        Yeah, well that's the past. You had your chance. She's happy bein' Mrs. Pauli
        Pittafora and your job now is takin' care of Vince's little girl. You ain't the boss yet,
        and it's our future too.

                              TONY
        I know. (sighs) OK, let's ace the lawyer and get out of these stinkin' swamps. I have
        a feelin' that Indian is gonna' lead us right to him

They head back to the fire, bed down.

                              TONY
                   (to himself, staring up at the cold stars)
        You almost got away with it, but I got Mary, and tomorrow, I'm gonna' kill your ass,
        and then it's all mine.

CUT TO:

EXT. BAYOU - DAWN

T.J. and Billy slogging through the swamp.

MONTAGE: T.J. makes as much NOISE as he can; splashing his feet through the water, bending branches back, snapping them towards Billy's head, and, unseen, TWISTING others. Billy struggles to keep up, an alien in a strange world; stumbling over loose rocks, ducking tree limbs, stopping frequently to shift his heavy pack, jerking T.J. to a halt.

WIDE: As T.J. leaps over a submerged log in a narrow stream. Billy tries the same maneuver but falls short, landing on the log:

                              BILLY
                   (as the "log" turns into a large submerged swamp turtle)
        Ooohhh!

And falls on his ass, into the stream, dropping T.J.'s leash. The turtle raises its sharp, curved beak, and takes a major bite out of Billy's arm.

                              BILLY
                         (in pain)
        Aggghhh! Goddam thing bit me!!

He scrambles for dear life up the bank, gripping his bleeding arm, sobbing in fright.

T.J. goes to Billy, slips off the backpack, opens it, takes out a T-shirt. Stripping off Billy's jacket and ripping his shirt sleeve, ties the T-shirt as a tourniquet.

                    T.J.
    Sit down, mister. You're losin' blood, and you might go into shock.

FOLLOW T.J. - Now free, he searches the shore, careful to avoid the angry turtle. Stooping, he pulls some reedy weeds, reaches under the water for a handful of mud. RETURNS to Billy, who is white-faced and glassy-eyed.

                    T.J.
    This ain't gonna' hurt...any more than you already are.

As T.J. breaks the reeds, releasing a milky liquid, squeezes it on Billy's lacerations, follows up with a mud covering. Removing the T-shirt from above the wound, he presses it directly on it, tying it tightly.

                    BILLY
              (wincing with pain)
    That hurts. God, I hate these fuckin' swamps!

                    T.J.
    You'll be OK for a while. Should get a tetanus shot.

                    BILLY
    Yeah, well I'll think about it, after I take care of my business.

He stands unsteadily, picks up the leash.

                    BILLY (cont.)
    Let's go, kid. I'm in a hurry

                    T.J.
    You're sure welcome, mister.

CUT TO:

EXT. BAYOU - LATER

Ed follows T.J.'s trail, keeping well behind so he's not seen. Comes across the stream, reads the disturbance, spots the blood. CONTINUES ON.

CUT TO:

Tony, Itsy and Sal behind Myron, following Ed's tracks. Myron STOPS, half-kneels, examines water-filled footprints.

                              MYRON
         Ed's up ahead. Must've changed his mind about huntin' the aspens. (duckwalking
         upstream) Somethin's weird; he seems to be stayin' behind someone else...two of
         'em, but I don't see no deer tracks anywhere.

Tony exchanges looks with the others.

                              TONY
         Keep on goin', kid. You're doin' good.

CUT TO:

EXT. BAYOU - EVENING - SAME

Billy, looking tired and weak, but hanging on grimly to T.J.'s leash, and cradling his mag pistol, sits on the ground, his back against a mangrove. T.J. sits opposite him, skinning a frog he's caught for dinner.

                              BILLY
         You actually going to eat that?

                              T.J.
         Sure. Tastes like chicken.

                              BILLY
                           (disgusted)
         That's all I hear down here. Rattlesnakes taste like chicken…armadillos taste like
         chicken, frogs too? Why the hell don't you just eat chicken?

T.J. smiles, runs a forked stick through frog and holds it over the tiny fire he's made.

                              T.J.
         I didn't see any chickens. Want some? Plenty more in the crick.

C.U. BILLY'S EYES Start to CLOSE from exhaustion. He WILLS them open - and sees T.J. looking at him, eating his frog, and smiling, the firelight glinting in his eyes.

CUT TO:

EXT. THE FOREST - SAME

ANGLE ON ED - High on a hill overlooking Billy and T.J.'s campsite, studying them through his binocs.

                              ED
                         (to himself)
         City boy's in bad shape. T.J.'s playin' him just right. Shouldn't be long now.

He HEARS something; cocks his head, trying to locate direction:

                              ED (cont.)
         Somebody comin'…who the hell now?...

Soundlessly, he slips off the hill, circling around and behind. STAY WITH HIM as he gains a vantage point and SEES; Myron and his group.

                              ED
                         (furious)
         What the fuck! Followin' me. That twerp can't find his ass with toilet paper. They're
         gonna' run right into T.J. and that killer. Gotta head 'em off

ANGLE ON ED - Intentionally noisy, makes his presence known, strikes off in the direction of the caves.

ON MYRON (thinks he hasn't been seen; low, to the others)

                              MYRON
         There he goes. Quiet now.

CUT TO:

EXT. THE CAVES - SAME

The Moon's disappeared behind thick clouds, and it's started to DRIZZLE.

ANGLE ON ED - Coming up, spots a large BROWN BEAR nosing around Myron's campsite, strewn with candy wrappers, empty beer bottles and remains of last night's dehydrated dinners. HEARING Myron's group a few minutes behind him, Ed reaches into his backpack, pulls out a fist-sized chunk of venison jerky. Aiming carefully, he fires the jerky low and fast into the cave Myron's group used last night. The bear, startled, lumbers after it.

ON MYRON and group as they move into the clearing, look around for Ed.

                              TONY
         You lost him, kid.

                    MYRON
No, I didn't. He just come in out of the rain for the night - in one of these caves, most likely. We'll pick him up in the mornin'.

                    SAL
I'm bushed, Tone. Gonna' crash inside.

                    ITSY
Me too. I'm cold, I don't need to be wet too.

All four troop into the cave. SECONDS LATER - A tremendous ROAR - yelling, a gun goes OFF - followed by Tony, Sal, Itsy & Myron exiting cave in a hurry. No sign of the bear.

ON ED - Enjoying it.

CUT TO:

INT. U.S.ATTORNEY'S OFFICE - LITTLE ROCK - DAY

MEETING IN PROGRESS - Between U.S. Attorney, HENRY GELDEN, and U.S. Marshals, Pierce and Butler.

                    GELDEN
He better not have disappeared. I'll bust both of you all the way back to game wardens.

                    PIERCE
Went out to see him, give him his money. He's gone...truck too.

                    BUTLER
Ain't been seen in town for a few days.

                    GELDEN
Only two possibilities. His Yankee friends caught up with him, or he's on the run.

                    PIERCE
Asked the local farmers about any fresh dirt mounds in their fields. He could've been dumped in the woods, we'd never know. What's your guess, Butler?

                    BUTLER
He lit out. What's a big-city mafia lawyer gonna' do 'round here anyway? Said he hates the food, the weather, the folks and the fishin'. Good riddance, I say.

                              GELDEN
Butler, you damned cracker! You were a hairball who owned a titty bar before I
made you a marshal. I swear, I'm 'bout ready to give up on you. (to Pierce) This is
federal, I'm bound by court order. You two are gonna' get him back, hear? I'm
runnin' for senate next year, and I surely don't need this. (to both) Now you get on
the horn to Highway Patrol and the locals. We're gonna' require an all-points and a
chopper.

                              PIERCE
No we don't, Henry. Let us'n the boys take care of it...it'll be good practice

                              GELDEN
Hell no! You keep your damned militia out of it. Don't you read the papers? You
wanna' play soldier, you do it on your own time.

Disappointed, the two Marshals nod, head for the door.

CUT TO:

EXT. BAYOU - EARLY MORNING DRIZZLE AND FOG.

FROM ABOVE TREELINE - LOOK DOWN ON Myron, Tony, Sal & Itsy - cold, wet and
miserable, slog single file along an animal trail. Myron FREEZES, POINTS: HIS POV - Through
the mist, 60 yards away, three DEER, a buck and two doe, their fatal flaw, curiosity, stand dead
still, ears pointed, staring at them.

                              MYRON
                       (silently mouths to Tony)
               Take the shot.

TONY Shakes his head, motions toward Sal, who shrugs it off. Myron looks at Itsy, who also
passes.

MYRON Confused, but anxious to please, raises his RIFLE, AIMS

                              TONY
                          (a shout)
NO!

As the deer scatter, Tony LUNGES forward, knocking Myron's rifle down.

                              MYRON
               Hey...what...

Sal comes forward, grabs Myron by the neck, as Itsy picks up the rifle.

>   TONY
>   Cuff him.

Sal produces a police-issue plastic wrist wire, locks Myron's hands together in front of him. Myron looks bewildered and terrified.

>   TONY
>   (his face right in Myron's)
>   OK, Myron. We're not hunters, in case you didn't notice. But we got something to
>   do in this rotten swamp, and you're gonna' help us. We got no interest in hurtin' you,
>   so go along, and you'll get your money.

Myron, wide-eyed, nods.

>   TONY (cont.)
>   Now, your coach is trailin' the guy we want. He's right behind him, but not closin'
>   in. I wanna' know why. (to Sal) Let him go, Sal, he'll be a good boy.

Sal releases a trembling Myron.

>   TONY (cont.)
>   You think you could get us out front of him without him knowing?

Myron nods quickly.

>   TONY (cont.)
>   OK, we're not goin' back to the caves tonight, that's what he'll expect. We're pushin'
>   on.

PULL BACK to HIGH VANTAGE as they continue on, stumbling and sliding along the wet and slippery path.

CUT TO:

EXT. - U.S. MARSHAL'S COMMAND POST OUTSIDE EL DORADO - DAY –

Located in a large, empty BARN on a deserted farm. WORKERS erect satellite dishes, other MARSHALS set up perimeter checkpoints, gas up swamp buggies and air-boats, park four-wheel drive trucks and jeeps. TWO TEAMS of anxious BLOODHOUNDS and their HANDLERS arrive in a VAN. SOUND OF HELICOPTER getting closer.

ANGLE ON SKY - Small DOT becomes DEA helicopter - LOOMS larger as it settles noisily down on the meadow near the barn.

INT. BARN - OTHER WORKERS install telephones, computers, copier, fax, arrange desks, tables and chairs.

ANGLE ON Pierce, Butler and Sheriff Raines, leaning over large table holding maps as they oversee and direct activities.

                    PIERCE
I'll go up in the chopper first, mark out the search grid. I suggest y''all assign the ground and water routes.

ON A TECHNICIAN

                    TECH
Mr. Pierce, we're settin' up the CT screen...take a look?

Pierce nods, goes off with tech. FOLLOW THEM to corner of barn, where a six-by-six video screen flashes patterns. A PICTURE of the helicopter emerges.

                    TECH
That's the security camera on the roof. Operates 360 degrees from inside.

ANOTHER PICTURE APPEARS from high above the bayou - TRAVELING OVER endless miles of treetops.

                    TECH
That'll be from the chase plane Mr. Gelden borrowed from customs -- Mitsubishi MU-2. Got an infrared heat-seeker...can locate anything with a temperature from a thousand feet.

                    PIERCE
I'm impressed - think I'll use that for the search.

                    TECH
I have a message for you.

He throws a switch on the control panel. Picture CHANGES - To U.S. Attorney Henry Gelden, in his OFFICE.

                GELDEN (onscreen)
I heard you were impressed, Pierce.

> PIERCE (smiles)
> Never more than now, Henry.

> GELDEN
> Then if you're all out of excuses...go get me that lawyer.

CUT TO:

EXT. BAYOU - LATER THAT DAY

As darkness descends, Billy and T.J. build a crude camp - sheltering themselves from the steady drizzle by erecting a porous roof of pine boughs over a small clearing they've made under a towering Douglas Fir.

T.J's job - building a fire: WATCH HIM scoop out dry pine needles from several inches below the wet surface, pulling moss and lichen off tree bark for tinder. He gently blows, and carefully stokes his smoldering mass into a smokey, but acceptable flame.

BILLY - Leaning against a tree, the worse for wear, but meaner and more determined than ever. Still holding T.J. on the leash, he barks:

> BILLY
> Hurry up, kid. I'm cold and wet, and I hurt. What's there to eat…oh, forget it.

T.J. just shakes his head, as if feeling sorry for his tormentor. He stands, goes over to Billy.

> T.J
> I'll get us some food, mister, but you gotta' trust me. I'm not goin' anywhere.

Billy nods wearily, lets go of the leash. T.J. picks up the handle, winds and cinches the 12-foot leash around his waist, and steps out of the firelight into the surrounding dark.

CUT TO:

EXT. THE BAYOU - SAME - POV FROM BEHIND ED - As he sees his chance. BILLY takes this opportunity to pee. Shifts his machine pistol, walks over to a large boulder, back to camera, does his thing.

C.U. ED - Edging forward cautiously, trying to decide how best to surprise Billy, and close the distance between himself and T.J. - when, hands cupped, T.J. RE-ENTERS frame.

> BILLY
> (still peeing, looks over his shoulder)
> Whadda' ya' got there?

                              T.J.
                       (holding them up)
        River Eels...babies, whole nest of them. Taste pretty good roasted.

                              BILLY
                       (looks sick, turns away)
             God, what next?

T.J. guts the baby eels with a sharp stone, thrusts long twigs lengthwise through them, jams two Y-shaped branches upright in the ground over the fire, and lays the eel brochettes across. The fat little river snakes begin sizzling immediately.

SMASH CUT:

Ed BURSTS through the brush, LEAPING over the fire toward T.J.

BILLY, SHOCKED, WHIPS around, grabbing for his gun. Fumbling for the safety and trying to aim at the fast-moving Ed, he's forgotten to replace his member. A comic sight, except for the murderous blast thirty 9-millimeter ACP slugs make tearing up the trees, stripping leaves and felling branches.

STILL ON BILLY - As the smoke slowly clears, he's alone in the devastated clearing, frantically trying to locate T.J. and the intruder. Stuffing himself back into his pants, he ducks low and out of the light.

CUT TO:

Deep in the bayou, down at the bottom of a glade, T.J. tends to Ed's wounded side

                              T.J.
                       (carefully examining)
             Bleedin' pretty heavy, dad, but there's an exit hole. Looks like it went all the way
             through.

                              ED
                         (in pain)
             Keep the pressure on it for a couple 'a minutes, then off, then on again. Then bind
             it up...it'll be OK.

T.J. looks dubious but does what his father wants.

CUT TO:

ANOTHER PART OF THE BAYOU - ON TONY AND GROUP.

They've heard the barrage of gunfire and are galvanized.

                    SAL
A C-note the Indian wasted him.

                    TONY
Damn! I hope not, I wanted to do it myself. (to Myron) C'mon, pimple-face, earn your dough.

Myron, eyes wide with terror, plunges on ahead.

BACK TO BILLY - Crawling through the underbrush, feels something on his palm, wet and sticky; lifts it to his face.

                    BILLY
                 (to himself)
Blood. I got the bastard. All I gotta' do is finish him and his kid, and I'm home free.

He continues following the bent branches and parted brush made by the retreating Ed and T.J.

INT. CABIN OF CUSTOMS PLANE - Pierce and PILOT mapping coordinates.

                    PILOT
This is the last leg of this grid. (he peers out through windshield at gathering storm clouds) Weather's lookin' bad, wind's up - maybe we should wait until tomorrow.

                    PIERCE (busy with his map)
Gives us a fifty-mile square. Should be enough. (looks up) No, we can't wait until tomorrow, there's a little boy in danger out there, we're stayin' up.

He picks up microphone.

                    PIERCE
                 (into mike)
Butler......

                    BUTLER
                 (filtered)
Yeah, Hank...what you need?

                    PIERCE
You makin' any progress?

                           BUTLER
                          (filtered)
         Uh, huh. Sent the Sheriff and one of the dog teams off on an airboat. I'm takin'
         the other out on the trail.

                           PIERCE
         OK, stay in touch - over.

EXT. THE SKY - SAME - Storm clouds merge, thunder rumbles ominously and streaks of lightning flash.

CUT TO:

EXT. SWAMP

LONG SHOT - An AIRBOAT, driven by Sheriff Raines, along with his deputy, Alex, a dog handler and a team of bloodhounds zooms across the shallow, grass-choked water.

DOPPLER EFFECT as airboat streaks across screen, its huge 600 HP aircraft engine's propeller screaming, disappears into the mangroves.

CUT TO:

EXT. ANOTHER PART of the bayou.

Butler's search party of Marshals, the other bloodhounds and their handler troop along a trail, the dogs baying, stopping and circling, confused by the many other human and animal scents.

CUT TO:

EXT. BAYOU - SAME

Tony, his associates, and Myron trying to catch up to Billy, Ed and T.J. They fight the growing wind.

Myron reads the bush like a newspaper, waves the others on.

CUT TO:

INT. CUSTOMS PLANE -

Bathed in an orange/yellow glow, as though the Sun is setting behind them.

                        PILOT

Marshal, the winds are too heavy - our airspeed's over 300. This plane's not built for this. I'm takin' her down.

                        PIERCE
                        (to pilot)

The hell you are...I'll shoot you first. You got that infrared sensor turned on?

                        PILOT
              (trying to control pitch - points to dash)

Yeah, this here's the screen…nothing much yet.....wait a minute, looks like some action.

INSERT: SCREEN - Lights up with dancing vertical spikes.

                        PILOT

Too many silhouettes, I can't figure out what it means.

                        PIERCE

Let's go down for a look-see.

Pilot eases the MU-2's wheel forward.

EXT. POV UP FROM THE GROUND -SAME - PLANE SKIMS LOW OVER THE SWAMP - WEAVING ERRATICALLY IN THE WIND

Pierce and pilot look down and out from their sides.

                        PIERCE

Lord o'mercy, would you look at that!

THEIR POV - Thousands of animals and birds, running, wading, flying low, trying to escape something - but what?

ACTION SHOTS - Deer leaping over berms, their white tails winking out as they disappear into the gloom -- Heron spread their giant wings, take running starts before flapping noisily into the air -- Alligators move slowly down the waterways, only their eyes and nostrils visible -- rabbits and squirrels madly darting in every direction.

INT. PLANE -SAME

                        PILOT
        What the hell is it?

He checks his rear-view mirror -

INSERT: In the darkening sky - an even darker FUNNEL CLOUD.

BACK TO PILOT - He turns around for a better look through the small rear window;

EXT. FROM THE AIR

                        PILOT
        Mother of God!

                        PIERCE
                 (picks up mike)
        Base...patch me through to Butler!

EXT. PLANE BANKS SHARPLY - NOW FLYING DIRECTLY INTO PATH OF TORNADO

BACK TO INT. PLANE

                        BUTLER
                 (V.O.filtered)
        Expectin' you.

                        PIERCE
        What's happening down there?

                        BUTLER
        Sheriff's comin' round to take us out in the airboat.

                        PIERCE
        Call in all patrols now! When you get back, set up a perimeter and dig in. We'll have to wait it out. Over.

PIERCE'S POV - Of the fast-approaching tower of whirling wind in front of them;

CUT TO:

EXT. SMALL POND - SAME - WIND ROILS THE SURFACE

The pond lies in a semi-clearing. At its far end, a half-dome, made of woven tree limbs and branches packed with mud, rises some three feet off the surface of the water.

SOUNDS of thrashing in the bush.

ANGLE ON - Ed and T.J. emerge from the forest. Leaning heavily on his son, Ed looks around, spots the half-dome –

                    ED
Beavers...C'mon, we'll be safe there.

FOLLOW THEM as they make their slow, painful way around the shore, arriving just behind the mound.

                    ED (cont.)
Walk backwards into the water...I'll hold on to your hands. When it gets up to your chin, duck under and come up inside...there's air in there.

                    T.J.
Dad, I don't know...I'm scared, you're bleeding again.

                    ED
Its all right to be scared, son. I am too, but we'll be OK, I've done this before. Just don't let go of me, understand?

T.J. nods, starts walking slowly backwards into the water, not taking his eyes off his father.

MED C.U. The water rising towards T.J.'s chin. His eyes mirror panic as his feet lose contact with the pond's bottom.

                    ED
Easy, you're doing fine. Now...Duck under! I won't let go of you!

ON T.J.'s FACE as it disappears beneath the surface.

BACK TO ED as he quickly follows.

INT. BEAVER LODGE

T.J. and Ed pop up, gasping for breath. Interior is a perfect hiding place; darkly shaded and larger than it looks from outside, with air circulating through its woven branches. They can see out, but can't be seen.

                        ED

You okay?

                        T.J.
                     (grinning)

Yeah, dad. This is cool! My buddies are gonna' freak when I tell them how you saved me, n'all.

Ed smiles.

                      T.J.(cont.)

You did this in Vietnam, huh? When are gonna' tell me about what you did there? You promised, dad.

                        ED

I know, son, and I will...someday, when you're older.

                    T.J. (disappointed)

You always say that.

CUT TO:

EXT. POND - MOMENTS LATER

Billy, coming out of the woods and onto the pond. He looks around, spots water-filled depressions in the mud that could be footprints, follows them to the other side, where they disappear.

INT. BEAVER LODGE - SAME

T.J., shivering from the cold water, trying to keep his teeth from chattering, looks over at Ed - his eyes are closed, and he's softly moaning in pain. T.J. reaches out, feels his dad's forehead...it's hot.

T.J. - Alerted by sounds from outside - peers out.

T.J.'s POV through the latticework - Billy, staring right at him!

Frightened, T.J. covers Ed's mouth...holds perfectly still.

BACK TO BILLY

Hasn't registered the beaver lodge, finally looks away. Baffled, he strikes off into the woods again.

CUT TO:

INT. BEAVER LODGE - SAME

Confident Billy's gone, T.J. struggles to pull his father under and through the water to the shore.

EXT. POND - SAME

Holding Ed's face out of the water, T.J. drags them both to land, sinks down, exhausted. The howling wind hurls tree limbs crashing through the forest, forcing T.J. to his feet. Gathering his strength, he helps his father up, and supporting him, they move off in the same direction as Billy. But this time, they're BEHIND him.

CUT TO: ANGLE - SAME

Billy, stumbling through the swamp, the billowing dust and leaves blinding him, comes to a river too wide to cross on foot. He looks around helplessly as muskrats, armadillos, possum, even a family of mule deer SCURRY past him, leap in, SWIM for the far shore. Wading in, holding his machine pistol above his head, he side paddles out.

CUT TO:

Tony's group, hurrying as fast as they can, the wind licking at their retreating boots.

> TONY
> (wiping his eyes, to Myron)
> Hey kid, we goin' in the right direction?

> MYRON
> (looks back through the haze at the funnel cloud low in the sky)
> Don't seem like we got much selection.

CUT TO:

EXT. FOREST - SAME

Marshals and deputies have dug in behind their vehicles and set up a perimeter at the forest's edge.

CUT TO:

EXT. BARN - MARSHAL'S COMMAND POST - SAME

POV from ground as Pierce's chase plane lands bumpily on the pasture, taxis past idling helicopter, shuts down.

ANGLE: Pierce deplanes, hurries into barn.

INT. BARN – SAME

                TECH
              (to Pierce)
Forest Service closed the area...says to call off the search.

               PIERCE
No shit. I'm goin' up in the chopper. Keep me updated.

EXT. PIERCE RUNNING TO HELICOPTER - SAME

ANGLE: Pierce pulls himself in; chopper starts to rise even before he's closed his door.

INT. HELICOPTER - SAME - WHAT PIERCE SEES

A hellish scene of roaring winds, broken trees, birds being hurled from the sky, burning embers shooting skyward and black desolation behind the fast-moving tornado.

CUT TO:

EXT.- SAME

Tony's group coming up on the river.

              MYRON
           (glancing back)
We need to get across it

Sal starts to tremble, nearly cries..

               SAL
Not me, I'm a city boy, I can't swim.

                    TONY
              (surprisingly tender)
     Itsy and me'll hold you up. Don't be afraid, you can do it.

They plunge in, start across. Sal flails as the water rises above his nose, endangering Tony and Itsy.

CUT TO:

INT. HELICOPTER - SAME

                    PILOT
              (struggling with the stick)
     I can't hold her...we're goin' down.

                    PIERCE
              (to pilot)
     Try to get me this side of the river.

Pilot leans into the stick; the chopper banks sharply, heading straight down.

EXT. DUSK -SAME

Helicopter bounces to the ground - up again a few feet, getting hung a few feet off the forest floor on an uprooted tree.

ANGLE: Pierce leaps the few remaining feet to the ground, clutching his walkie-talkie.

ON PIERCE: He looks around, sees: TORN CORPSES of animals that couldn't outrun the wind - deer, marsupials, and caught in the frantic act of trying to dig itself a burrow, what was once a black bear.

C.U. - HE REACTS - Then sets off across the destroyed forest floor, through stripped skeletons of trees.

CUT TO:

EXT. - SAME

T.J. and Ed struggle to the edge of the river. T.J. looks back: the funnel cloud is right behind them, weaving to and fro like a gigantic cobra, but seemingly stalled. He gently sits his semi-conscious father on the ground, leaning against a large rock.

                              T.J
            Gotta' get us across somehow, daddy. Be right back.

MONTAGE: Searching the shoreline, he selects seven rotting, weakened lodge pole pines. Throwing himself against them, they lean further toward the water, within his reach. He jumps, grabs the tops, and pulls down until they snap off. Dragging the poles to the water, T.J. lines six up touching each other, and races back into the still-unharmed forest. He reaches a tall oak nearly encircled by strangler vines.

ANGLE FROM BELOW - Shinnying ten feet up the trunk, using the coiled creeper as steps, he rips the vine off, circling and unwinding as he descends. Back on the ground, T.J. loops the vine around his elbow and palm, runs back to the poles. Although Ed's wound is bleeding again, his eyes are open and he's breathing heavily.

                              T.J.
                          (to himself)
            Alright...at least he's awake.

MONTAGE: Working as fast as he can, T.J. ties the poles together into a crude raft, pushes it partly into the water. Running back to his father, he helps him onto the raft, laying him flat, piling their gear aboard. Leaping to shore, he grabs the last pole, and pushes the raft off into the heaving current.

                              T.J.
            Hang on, daddy we're goin' home.

Poling the flimsy, leaking raft against the wind and current would be tough for a man. T.J. struggles to keep them afloat and in the center of the fast-moving water.

HIGH ANGLE: The little raft drifting away, getting smaller and smaller until it's lost in the distance.

CUT TO:

EXT. PERIMETER - SAME

The Sheriff's overloaded airboat skims off the water, bumps heavily over land - stops near the parked chase plane, its huge engine whining down.

ON PASSENGERS - Streaming off -

Sheriff Raines is last; he limps, surprisingly fast, over toward Butler, and other LAWMEN, studying a map stretched over the hood of a Forest Service fire pumper.

ANGLE ON CINDY - standing apart from the group. Buster veers to her first,

                    CINDY
                  (urgently)
Buster...they're in there. I'm going to lose them both!

                    BUSTER
Hell no you're not! Ed and me been in worse firefights. You just hang here, Cindy. I'll work this out.

He goes over to the lawmen.

                    BUSTER
Where's Pierce?

                    BUTLER
                (looks up, no love lost)
He put down behind the tornado, comin' this way, lookin' for your friend and his kid.

                    BUSTER
But Ed and T.J. are in there between the killers and the wind. Pierce can't help them from where he is.

                    BUTLER
You got a better idea, Sheriff?

                    BUSTER
I'm goin' in from this side.

                    BUTLER
Through the tornado? You're one crazy sonofabitch, Raines.

But the Sheriff is already halfway way back to the airboat.

THE AIRBOAT - SAME

Buster climbs on, fires up the engine, the propeller's back draft flattening the seven foot-high pampas grass behind it. GUNNING it, he ROARS past the startled faces of the other lawmen at the command post, only to YANK back on the stick as he sees Cindy standing defiantly right in FRONT of him.

                    BUSTER
              (yells at top of his voice)
      Damn it, Cindy, get away from there!

                    CINDY
              (yells back up at him)
         I'm goin'!

Seeing he has no choice, he leans over, grabs her hand, pulls her up next to him - and plunges INTO the howling winds.

FROM BEHIND THE SHERIFF PILOTING THE AIRBOAT

Like a Sunday drive through HELL - Intense wind ignites huge trees like fireworks; their groaning, cracking, death noises reverberate like cannon shot.

MONTAGE: With the airboat floating several inches off the ground, Buster skillfully navigates the unstable, overpowered platform through, and around still-standing trees, huge rocks and hundreds of oncoming fleeing animals and birds. No windshield or roof to protect them, they duck overhanging branches and firebrands shooting through the air, but Buster misses seeing a large black crow that HITS him smack in the face and bounces off. Losing control, he piles the air boat up between a big rock and a tree.

                    BUSTER
      Oh, fuck!...just what I need! I'll push - you steer!

With no reverse gear, Buster jumps off, runs around the front, starts pushing the heavy craft far enough back off the rocks to turn around, as Cindy leans over hard on the control stick.

Satisfied he has clearance, Buster starts to climb up again...feels something strange - looks down; a large animal TRAP clamped around his wooden prosthesis through his pants leg.

                    BUSTER
              (more angry than scared)
        Shit! That godamned L'aborteaux...it's all his fault.

Pulling on his wooden leg trying to free it proves futile. He starts stripping his pants off, hopping up and down on the ground.

BUSTER

Dammit! Second leg he's cost me! I'll rip his face off...

ANGLE ON CINDY

Despite their danger, she can't help smiling ruefully at Buster's predicament.

Unable to get his pants over his cowboy boots, Buster hoists himself up on the airboat deck, pulls off his boots, his pants, and finally, unbuckles his LEG, throwing it far off into the forest. Yanking his one boot back on, Cindy moves over, as he settles into the driver's seat and they ROAR on ahead.

CUT TO:

EXT. FOREST - SAME

Having made it across the river, Billy struggles through the blinding winds.

BILLY
(exhausted - to himself)
They're here somewhere...gotta' find 'em.....kill 'em.

CUT TO:

EXT. RIVER BANK - SAME

Tony's group has also made it to the other side. Although upright, Sal looks like he drowned. The effort to get this far has cost them their long guns and hunting paraphernalia. Armed only with semi-automatic pistols, they fight their way through the thick smoke.

CUT TO:

THE RIVER - SAME

Ed and T.J.'s little raft has bumped ashore at a rocky inlet too narrow to float through.

T.J. helping his father, who has recovered somewhat by resting, up and off the raft. He shoulders Ed's backpack and crossbow - looks around.

ED
We're behind the funnel now, son. You're a hell of a navigator.

T.J. couldn't be prouder, and shows it on his red face.

EXT. FOREST FLOOR - DAY

Myron leads Tony, Sal and Itsy through the broken wilderness, following depressions in the inch or two of debris that now covers the ground. Squatting, he studies the indentations:

> MYRON
> It's not the same guy we were following before.

> TONY
> That's OK, kid; just get us there without him catchin' on.

CUT TO:

EXT. MORAINE FIELD - SAME

A large, jumbled expanse of blackened boulders, some bigger than automobiles -- the 10,000 year-old remains of a retreating Ice Age glacier.

ANGLE ON Billy, near collapse, rests between two boulders wedged against each other, forming a natural cave. Sensing something, he SNAPS his MAC-10 up:

ANGLE ON A PUMA, not 10 yards away, unhurt and unruffled, stares at him. A moment passes; the big cat looks away, resumes its stealthy journey through the landscape, hunting for an opportunistic meal. WATCH THE PUMA pick at carcass of a rodent, before deciding it wants something less dead, and slowly evaporates into the mist, as though Billy had dreamed it.

CUT TO:

EXT. CREST OF A HILL - SAME

Pierce - lying flat to avoid being seen, glasses the area.

INSERT: PIERCE'S POV THROUGH BINOCS

In the distance, clouds of gray-black smoke, and the rear of the retreating tornado. Closer in, perhaps a half-mile away, easily seen in the denuded moonscape - Tony and his group.

> PIERCE
> (to himself)
> Hunters...got caught out and survived. But, shit! They're gonna' run into my man.

He stands, hurries down off the hill to get between this group and his quarry.

CUT TO:

EXT. AERIAL VIEW - BAYOU

T.J. and Ed, following the CURVE of the RIVER

They have unknowingly narrowed the distance between themselves, Tony's group and Billy, and are now very CLOSE.

Myron has brought Tony, Sal and Itsy to a point just BEHIND the moraine field. Finger to his lips, he points, whispers:

MYRON
Footprints end here. The fella' you want's probably holed up in them rocks.

Tony gestures to Sal and Itsy to quietly circle around - that he'll go straight, toward the rocks.

Pointing his pistol at Myron's head, he motions Myron to sit still, and not make a sound. Sal and Itsy FAN OUT.

CUT TO:

EXT. BAYOU - SAME

FROM A DISTANCE - The Sheriff's airboat bumps along the rock-strewn uneven ground.

The craft's flat, aluminum bottom has become superheated, and Buster's having trouble keeping his one good leg on the floor. Cindy has drawn her legs up, jamming her feet against the dash.

BUSTER
Ow...ow...goddamn it!

Buster makes wide, sweeping, figure-eights in his search for Ed and T.J.

LOW ANGLE

Sal, as inept in the woods as he would be on a dance floor, stumbles, nearly falling over loose gravel - grabs onto side of large boulder. Breathing heavily - sure he's been heard. The only SOUND now - the tinkle of dislodged gravel still traveling downhill.

ON BILLY - Alerted again.

> BILLY
> (to himself)
> Must be that mountain lion back again...

He flattens himself against rock wall, and waits.

ON TONY - His face contorted in fury at Sal's clumsiness, motions Itsy on, hunches down, continues toward the boulders.

BACK ON Sal - tense, edges around boulder, his eyes darting back toward Tony, and forward to the unknown. Trying for silence, nevertheless, Sal's bulk crunches the leaves and twigs.

ON BILLY - Waiting, pistol cocked.

CLOSE ON Sal's FACE

Fear, for maybe the first time in his life, as the cold barrel of Billy's MAC-10 comes up under, just touching Sal's chin.

PULL BACK - As Billy grabs Sal's 9mm. pistol away from him, jams it in his belt, pulls Sal into cave, throws him down, stepping on his neck.

> BILLY
> Who the fuck are you?

CUT BACK TO TONY

His disgusted look makes it clear he needs a new plan - and fast! Motioning to Itsy to stay where he is, behind and out of Billy's line of sight, Tony ducks behind a large tree trunk.

TWO-SHOT

> SAL
> (near tears)
> Don't kill me...don't...

> BILLY
> (hot)
> Why the fuck not? Why're you following me? Who's with you?

                    SAL
I'm just a hunter...got caught out.

                    BILLY
Yeah, sure...with this popgun. Where you from with that accent...New York, Jersey? Talk to me, asshole!

                    SAL
               (blubbering)
Philly....I'm from Philly!

BILLY - Slightly relaxed, but still doubtful.

                    BILLY
You better be.

CUT TO:

Ed and T.J., halting, to rest, at edge of forest, the moraine field stretching in front of them.

THEIR ANGLE - On cluster of boulders. ED'S POV: Billy, holding Sal at gunpoint.

                    ED
               (sotto voce)
The Sonofabitch got some other innocent hostage...listen, T.J., I'm goin' in to help. I want you to stay here, out of sight.

                    T.J.
               (alarmed)
No, dad...you can't...you're wounded.

                    ED
I'm OK! Now don't you move...I mean it!

CLOSE ON T.J.'s face - fear and frustration.

Ed, crouching low, clutching his rifle, and clearly masking his pain, sets out on a zigzag course closer to the action.

ANOTHER ANGLE - SAME

Pierce, running as fast as he can through the debris, trips over a log, falls heavily on his ankle.

>   PIERCE
> Damn!
>   (reaches for his walkie-talkie)
>   Butler! Butler!

CUT TO:

COMMAND POST - SAME

INTERCUT:

>   BUTLER
>   (phone to his ear)
> Yeah, Hank, where are you?

>   PIERCE
> Down...twisted my damn ankle...seen anything?

>   BUTLER
> Fuck, no! Just a buncha' animals n'birds, and a shitload of wind. Want us to
> fly you out?

>   PIERCE
> No! All Hell's gonna' break loose, I need to be on the ground. Keep this line open.

He painfully stands, limps on.

CUT TO:

CLOSE ON TONY - SAME

His frustration overruling his reason, he suddenly leaps out from behind his tree, SHOUTS:

>   TONY
>   L'ABORTEAUX!

WHIP CUT TO: CLOSE ON BILLY'S FACE

SURPRISED and CONFUSED at being called out by that name.

                    BILLY
                (to himself)
    L'aborteaux? They must think I'm him.
                    (to Sal, still spread-eagled on the ground)
        Know who that is, asshole?

                    SAL
                (muffled, his mouth in the dirt)

No...

                    BILLY
                (to himself)
    Maybe a rescue party. At least they're not lookin' for Billy Rubin.
                    (to Sal)
        Don't move, schmuck!

BILLY slowly emerges from behind the boulder, moves into view, looking for the source of the voice.

                    BILLY
        Yeah...who wants me?

SMASH CUT: On Tony, out in the open, his pistol extended.

                    TONY
                (a deadly grin)
        I do, motherfucker!

QUICK CUT BACK TO BILLY

                    BILLY
                (shocked)
        Tony Greco? (then he smiles) Shit, why not!

Billy snaps his MAC-10 up -

Tony squeezes off three hurried shots; one hits Billy in the knee, spinning him halfway around.

Billy - grimacing in pain, drops to his good knee, pulls his trigger.

INSERT: MAC-10 on full auto, spitting out flame and smoke.

Tony - hit, and hit again...drops like a rock, rolling down into a glade.

                    BILLY
          Got ya', you dago sonofabitch!

Still on the ground, Billy whips around, sees Sal climbing to his feet - takes AIM.

ANOTHER ANGLE

Other side of Billy's boulder.

CLOSE ON ITSY

                    ITSY
          Don't shoot...we give...

Hands raised, comes out from hiding.

                    BILLY
               (turns around, ready to fire)
          I know you, don't I?

                    ITSY
          Yeah...we work for Tony and his old man.

                    BILLY
          Well now you work for me. Tony's dead, and Vince and Ray are in jail for life. I'm going back and takin' over. Put your gun away. You and your friend go dig a hole for that shithead over there.

Itsy and Sal exchange looks of amazement at the change in their fortunes, move off down the glade to bury Tony.

ANGLE ON Ed, breaking cover BEHIND the now-alone Billy -- stands unsteadily, his rifle wavering.

                    ED
          Freeze...Don't move!

ON BILLY'S BACK - He slowly raises his hands - the MAC held high.

Itsy and Sal - Down in the glade with Tony's body, look at each other -- now what?

ANGLE IN FRONT OF BILLY - CLOSE on his face - Eyes darting, thinking furiously.

PULL BACK - As Ed's legs come into view behind the still-seated Billy.

Through his pain, Billy half-turns, reaches behind him, grabs Ed's legs, yanking him to the ground. The two wounded men struggle for the weapons.

CUT TO:

Itsy and Sal abandon Tony's body, start climbing back up.

FROM A DISTANCE - SAME

The Sheriff's airboat CRASHES through the brush, into the moraine field.

BUSTER'S POV:

Ed and Billy locked in a death struggle; but CLOSER to him, just coming over the hill, Itsy and Sal, guns drawn.

BUSTER drags the control stick over, spinning the airboat around, using the prop wash, blasting Itsy and Sal back, and over the precipice, where they tumble to the bottom.

ON ED AND BILLY

Ed's wound has opened up again, and he's losing blood. Weakened, he's no match for the enraged Billy, who has the upper hand, and gotten possession of Ed's rifle. Raising it high, about to smash the butt into Ed's face;

ANGLE ON T.J.

Racing to his father's aid - shudders to a halt with the only weapon he has - raises the crossbow and FIRES.

CLOSE ON BILLY - SLO-MO:

The six-inch bolt, with its triangular, serrated tip smashes into Billy's upper right shoulder, just below his collarbone, making a grinding noise, as it saws through the bone.

REVERSE

The tip extrudes a good half-inch through Billy's scapula.

BILLY - His eyes wide in surprise - drops the MAC-10 - still on full auto, it hits the ground, jumping around as it empties its magazine, bullets flying in every direction.

SILENCE - As the last echo of gunfire dies away.

CUT TO:

AIRBOAT

Sal and Itsy, covered by Buster's shotgun, stand still, hands on head.

CINDY jumps off airboat - dashes to her husband and child - lift's Ed's head into her lap, hugging T.J.

NEW ANGLE - Pierce, still limping, out of breath, arrives at the boulders, looks around.

> PIERCE
> (to Ed)
> Who're you?

> ED
> Ed L'aborteaux
> (inclines his head toward Billy).
> You know this guy?

> PIERCE
> Yeah, he's Ed L'aborteaux too. At least until we find out who he really is.

ON BILLY - Glaring, badly wounded, but he'll live.

ED - Looks over at Buster.

> ED
> (to Pierce)
> Better go give the Sheriff a hand. Don't know how they were dumb enough to hire a one-legged lawman anyhow.

> BUSTER
> (from a distance)
> Sit on my stump, you damned Indian!

PIERCE calls in on his walkie-talkie.

> PIERCE
> Butler? Get that medi-vac chopper airborne, pronto!

Goes over to airboat, handcuffs Sal and Itsy.

CUT TO:

FOREST EDGE - SAME

Myron, hands up, emerges, looking like he's seen Hell and Redemption all at once.

> ED
> Hey, just the man I want to see. C'mon over here, Myron. I'm pissed, you ruined my huntin'.

> MYRON
> (thinks he means it)
> I'm sorry, Ed.
> (looks at Billy)
> Guess I don't get my money, huh?

> T.J.
> Real brainy, Myron, and soon as my dad's OK, you lose your job too.

> ED
> (looks up at Cindy, smiles)
> Don't know about that, son. Your momma says I need to take some time off...maybe go to church with you.

ON T.J.'S BEAMING FACE - CUT TO:

POV: SKY - SAME

Medi-vac helicopter settles down with a ROAR. Two paramedics jump down; begin attending to Billy and Ed.

                    FIRST PARAMEDIC
Chopper's got two strut stretchers, these the only two wounded?

Before Pierce can answer -

                         ED
                   (looking at Billy)
I'm not sharing the same airspace with him. I'll ride back with the Sheriff.

                   SECOND PARAMEDIC
You look pretty bad, mister. You sure? We got room inside.

                         ED
                  (grimacing with pain)
I been hurt worse, I'll make it.

                    FIRST PARAMEDIC
OK, it's your funeral. Anybody else need a ride?

                       PIERCE
Yeah, I'll take the prisoners with me. You can put their former boss on the other strut. (He leans over to Billy) You don't mind ridin' with Tony? I don't think he cares.

CHOPPER, BLADES WHIRLING –

Paramedics first lift Billy to strut stretcher, strap him on, then do the same with Tony's body and climb back into helicopter.

ON PIERCE, ED AND BUSTER

                       PIERCE
                       (to Ed)
Well, I guess you're the only one using your name now.

                         ED
                      (furious)
How do I know that? Are you gonna' tell the FBI, or am I, that they can't just let criminals choose any damned name they want when they're hiding out.

                              PIERCE
            Wouldn't make much difference either way, would it? Just wasn't your lucky day.

Pierce turns away, oversees handcuffed Sal and Itsy and Myron being loaded aboard, hoists himself up.

Helicopter lifts, noses off.

CUT TO:

EXT. AIRBOAT - SAME

Buster slides over, making room for T.J., Ed and Cindy.

                              BUSTER
            You drive, T.J.
                      (to Ed)
            We had this machine back in 'Nam, we would've won that war by ourselves.

                              T.J.
                      (to Buster)
            You mean it? But I'm not old enough...and...and I don't know how.

                              BUSTER
            Well, whatever you do, don't tell the Sheriff. Besides, it's time you learned.
                      (to Ed)
            That reminds me, you owe me a new leg!

LATER - Back on water, cruising slowly, if erratically, under T.J.'s control, down a vegetation-choked channel.

MED. WIDE

                              ED
                      (to Cindy)
            Maybe I'm just glad to be alive, but I'm seein' things a little different now.

Buster looks over, smiles.

                              ED (cont.)
                      (although it's painful, he stretches to put his arms around her and T.J.)
            The only thing that's real is family. I'm double blessed with the two of you. Don't see why we shouldn't extend it. (to T.J) I think it's time we had that talk.

ON T.J.'S GRIN - PULL BACK TO AERIAL

CAMERA RISES - airboat and its occupants become smaller and smaller, until it becomes part of the bayou, and disappears.

FADE OUT

www.ingramcontent.com/pod-product-compliance
Lightning Source LLC
Chambersburg PA
CBHW051406070526
44584CB00023B/3316